BURLINGTON

THE GROWING YEARS

The paintings on the covers of this book are reproductions of works by Paul Duff done especially for the Burlington Historical Society.

Born in Hamilton, Paul Duff is a world traveller. He has painted and taught in Switzerland, Brazil and Burlington. He is now enjoying life in his new home on the Bruce Peninsula. The Burlington Historical Society thanks him for his generous contribution.

BURLINGTON

THE GROWING YEARS

by
DOROTHY TURCOTTE

THE BURLINGTON HISTORICAL SOCIETY

Canadian Cataloguing in Publication Data

Turcotte, Dorothy, 1929-
  Burlington: the growing years

Includes bibliographical references and index.
ISBN 0-9696575-0-1

1. Burlington (Ont.) - History.   I. Burlington
Historical Society.   II. Title.

FC3099.B87T87   971.3'533   C92-095307-7
F1059.5.B87T87 1992

Pictures with no credit given are those of the Burlington
Historical Society.

Published by:
THE BURLINGTON HISTORICAL SOCIETY
3062 Woodward Avenue
Burlington, Ontario
L7N 2M2
(416) 637-8000

Produced by:
AMPERSAND PRINTING
123 Woolwich Street
Guelph, Ontario
N1H 3V1
(519) 836-8800

The Burlington Historical Society wishes to acknowledge the
financial support and encouragement of the Ministry of National Health & Welfare Canada (New Horizons), the Ontario
Ministry of Culture & Communications, and the City of Burlington.

TABLE OF CONTENTS

ACKNOWLEDGEMENTS

In 1988 and 1989, when the book committee of the Burlington Historical Society worked with me to publish *Burlington: Memories of Pioneer Days*, the book was planned to include families who settled in Wellington Square, the village of Burlington, and the surrounding communities that are now included in Burlington from approximately 1780 to 1900. *Burlington: The Growing Years* is a continuation of that chronicle, covering much of this century.

Some of the families in this book are familiar names from the previous volume, for inevitably some pioneer families continued to contribute to the development of Burlington from village to town, from town to city. Others are families who took advantage of our increasingly mobile 20th century society to come here, and thus use their talents to enrich the community.

As with *Burlington: Memories of Pioneer Days*, most of the research was done by members of the book committee who spent many hours interviewing, making notes, selecting photographs, and organizing the format. It has been my job to put all of this into a written form which I trust the reader will find interesting. Once again, it has been a pleasure to work with this knowledgeable group of people which includes book committee chairman Irma Coulson, and committee members Mary Fraser, Florence Meares, Ruth Borthwick, and John Borthwick. My personal thanks also go to Marion Jackson (Alton), Betty O'Hara (Breckon), Kate Krenz (Coleman), Ida Reddy, Shirley Bottaro (Hunt), Paul Almas, Ruth Simmons (Almas) and Archdeacon Homer Ferris who provided me with information, in addition to that obtained by the historical society. Thanks, also, to Fred Oldfield without whose help I would never have learned the intricacies of the computer, and thus put this book together with considerably less difficulty than I experienced in using a computer for the first time with the previous volume.

Dorothy Turcotte

The Book Committee of The Burlington Historical Society is grateful to the following people who have generously contributed information and pictures. Without them this book would not have been possible.

If, inadvertently, any name has been omitted from this list, the error is sincerely regretted.

Alderson, Howard, Burlington
Almas, Paul, Burlington
Alton, Doug, Burlington
Armstrong, May & Frank, Burlington
Atkins, Mary, Lindsay
Bateman, Robert, Fulford Harbour, B.C.
Bell, Bonita & Harris, Milton
Borthwick, Ruth, Burlington
Bottaro, Shirley, Grimsby
Brandon, Phyllis, Burlington
Campbell, Mary & Glen, Milton
Chetter, Margaret, Burlington
Cleaver, Ivan, Burlington
Coleman, Brant, Burlington
Cooke, Bill, Burlington
Coulson, Irma, Milton
Crans, Jackie, Burlington
DeBruin, Hubert, Burlington
Dixon, Laura, Milton
Ferris, Archdeacon Homer, Hamilton
Fiamelli, Joe & Lee, Burlington
Ghent, Elsie, Sudbury
Gibson, Donald, Burlington
Goodbrand, Dr. James, Burlington
Gudgeon, Vicki & Eric, Milton
Harrow, Flossie, Burlington
Hawley, George, Burlington
Hellingman, Meta & Thomas, Burlington
Homer, John, Burlington
Howard-Lock, Helen, Burlington
Hunter, Margaret, Burlington
Jackson, Marion, Ridgetown
Job, Rendell, Burlington
Johnston, Jewel, Burlington
Krenz, Kate, Lakefield
Langford, Helen, Ganges, B.C.
Lindley, Bruce, Burlington
Lindley, Peter, Ancaster

Love, Dr. William, Burlington
Marshall, Annette, Hamilton
Martin, Alfreda, Burlington
McKeen, Isabel, Burlington
Meares, Florence, Burlington
Millward, George, Burlington
Morton, Jean, Burlington
Norton, Alan, Burlington
O'Dell, Margaret, Burlington
O'Hara, Elizabeth, Vineland
Oldfield, Fred, Grimsby
Peart, Murray, Etobicoke
Pettit, Murray, Burlington
Posavad, Frances, Burlington
Reddy, Ida, Hamilton
Reinhardt, Muriel, Burlington
Richardson, Mabel, Burlington
Ritchie, Anne, Burlington
Robinson, Edna, Burlington
Sharp, Mary, Burlington
Simmons, Ruth, Hamilton
Sinclair, Dr. Gordon, Toronto
Slavin, Alice, Niagara-on-the-Lake
Smith, Floss, Peterborough
Sovereign, Suzanne, Belleville
Swan, Mary, Burlington
Tuck, Beulah, Burlington
Turcotte, Dorothy, Grimsby
Virtue, Dr. Jack, Burlington
Weber, Mary Jane, Burlington
Wickens, Stan, Waterdown
Wingfield, Anne, Burlington
Wright, Mary, Burlington
Other Sources:
The Burlington Post
The Burlington Spectator
The Hamilton Public Library, Special
  Collections
The Ontario Provincial Archives

PREFACE

Peter Newman, an ex-Burlington resident and one of the most interesting current historical writers in Canada, has written, "It is personal encounters that make history, which is no more than memories refined, come alive." That is exactly what the Book Committee of the Burlington Historical Society has tried to do in this second volume on families who played a part in the history of Burlington. The Book Committee members plumbed the memories of many local residents. The story strands we provided were then woven by Dorothy Turcotte into an interesting and informative history of this community in the 20th Century.

Book Two should be a required companion book to our first effort, *Burlington: Memories of Pioneer Days*.

Again, the many hours spent in interviewing, reading notes, collecting pictures and maps have seemed endless. I would like to thank the Book Committee members, Irma Coulson, chairperson, Mary Fraser, Florence Meares, and Ruth Borthwick. Thanks also to the members of the Burlington Historical Society who helped in various ways, and to the interviewees who co-operated so graciously. Special thanks are in order to Katherine Clifton and Edna Phillips who also proofread the manuscript.

Our gratitude as an Historical Society goes out to the Provincial Ministry of Culture and Communications, the New Horizons Program of the Ministry of National Health and Welfare and the federal Ministry of Citizenship and Culture for their financial aid which has made this book possible.

John W. Borthwick, President
Burlington Historical Society

TURN-OF-THE-CENTURY
BURLINGTON

As the 19th century turned into the 20th, the village of Burlington was still a small, rural community. The business district on Brant Street stretched almost as far north as the site of to-day's city hall. Beyond that on Brant Street were the gracious fruit farms that gave the village its popular designation as The Garden of Canada.

Yet the "downtown" focus had changed, from the bustling industry of shipping to that of placid commerce amid an agricultural district. In 1900, street lighting came to the central part of the village. Automobiles had not yet become a familiar sight, and iron rings were still on curbs and posts so that citizens could hitch their horses safely while in town on business.

Children could still cut through woods and fields to reach Burlington Central Public School. When school was out, they rambled at will, even playing hopscotch, skipping or roller skating on the streets where traffic was minimal. Neither parents nor young people worried about the dangers of allowing such freedom, for those were the days when everyone in town was a relative, or at least a friend!

Burlington was famous throughout Ontario for the fine fruit and vegetables produced on its excellent soil. Aldershot melons, Maple Avenue tomatoes, Nelson Township peaches and cherries were sought after in stores in Toronto and farther afield because everyone knew that they were of highest quality and flavour. Many of the innovations in fruit and vegetable growing sprang from Burlington farms. New varieties were created; new methods tested and proven. Some farmers took a special interest in the agricultural associations which were coming into being, and made outstanding contributions to their development and achievements.

As the century wore on, things changed, gradually at first. By the 1940s, the Brant Street business district had expanded.

Farms were beginning to disappear, to be replaced by residential developments, and on the outskirts of town, industries. By the time Burlington became a city in 1973, the changes became more rapid and more obvious.

As we approach the 21st century, Burlington has grown from a village with only a few hundred inhabitants into a modern city with a population of 129,500. Imagine the amazement of William Kerns, reeve in 1900, and his village council if they could be set down in today's city, to marvel at the changes that have taken place!

I

AGRICULTURE

Early settlers everywhere immediately set up farms in order to support their families' basic needs. However, only in areas where the soil was sufficiently fertile did farming become an industry. Those who came to the Burlington area were fortunate, for the surrounding soil, once cleared of trees, proved to be excellent. Wheat, orchard fruits, small fruits and vegetables all grew abundantly with the result that many well-known family farms were handed down from generation to generation.

In the late 1800s and early 1900s, Burlington farmers became pioneers in successfully shipping and exporting perishable fruits through the use of cold storage. Thus the town became famous, not only within Canada but abroad as well, for its excellent produce.

To-day, commercial development, highways and housing have buried most of the rich soil that once was Burlington's greatest claim to fame.

LINDLEY, Robert

Robert Lindley came to Canada with his parents and siblings when he was 12 years old. First, the family lived in a log house near Mount Nemo, and later on a farm on what is now the North Service Road, so Robert grew up in a farming family. As a young man, he worked as a farm labourer for Joshua Freeman on the old Ghent farm.

When Benjamin Eager offered property for sale on Sand Road (now Maple Avenue) in 1873, Robert Lindley was the first buyer. He purchased 70 acres on the west side of the road, paying $63 per acre. Many thought the land would not produce anything, but within five years, Lindley had sold 28 acres for more than he paid for the entire 70. On the remaining property, he planted orchards, and also grew small fruits, vegetables, and grain for cattle feed. Robert's home is still standing, in good repair, at 562 Maple Avenue.

Robert's brother, Joseph, also had property on Sand Road. Joseph and his wife Hattie (nee Harriet Emery) had four children, but only the youngest, James Arthur (Art) lived beyond childhood. When Art married Annie Thorpe in 1899, the newlyweds moved into the family home with Joseph and Hattie. Annie promptly took charge of things. She was known as a bundle of energy, and an astute manager. She gradually expanded the orchards and small fruit plantings, while diminishing the livestock on the farm, except for the horses which her husband loved. The farm grew delicious melons, and Art loved to share one with his grandchildren.

For many years, Art was the assessor for Nelson Township, and knew the area better than anyone else. Everyone knew when Art was in the vicinity, for he constantly jingled the change in his pocket.

Produce from the farm was taken regularly to Hamilton market, and often was shipped by rail to Toronto from Freeman or the station at the foot of Maple Avenue. When Art's son Martin bought a Reo truck, shipments were delivered as far away as Orillia.

In 1930, greenhouses were built to speed the growing season. Gradually, small fruits were replaced by tomatoes, potatoes, cabbage, lettuce, asparagus, celery and cauliflower. Apples, pears and cherries continued to flourish on the farm. Sour cherries were sold to Mammy's Bread in Hamilton for pies.

In 1931, at the height of the Depression, in an effort to find an outlet for their farm produce, the Lindleys got in touch with the purchasing department of a new chain of grocery stores, Dominion Stores Limited. As a result of this contact, Dominion Stores became a market for most of the produce grown on the farm for the next 40 years.

In 1935, Martin and his brother, Bruce, formed a partnership under the name Lindley's Fruits and Vegetables. This partnership was continued by Martin's son, Peter, and Bruce's son, David, until the farm was sold for development in 1973. At that time, Peter and David moved their operation to An-

net Marshall, later Lindley,
n front) behind Brant Inn,
:ound 1923.
-Courtesy Helen Lindley Langford

iady Cottage — Fisher Home — now the site of Burlington Mall.

caster. In 1961, Peter was instrumental in forming Skyway Brand Growers, a marketing co-op made up of several growers.

David's wife, Jane Lindley, recalls an incident which she refers to as part of "the joy of farming on Maple Avenue." One windy spring night, the plastic greenhouses were blowing noisily. At two a.m., Jane and David were awakened by Peter shouting at the top of his lungs for David to hurry outside. When they looked out of the window, they saw Peter silhouetted against yards and yards of plastic which had been ripped loose by the wind.

The western 25 per cent of the Maple Avenue property became the northern portion of what is now the Mapleview Mall. The rest became the section of Fairview Street running from the Queen Elizabeth overpass east to the new Burlington Central Fire Station, with the Longo plaza on the north side of the street and The Brownstones residential development on the south.

FISHER, William

William Fisher and his bride, Sarah Allan, took up residence at Shady Cottage on the Guelph Line in 1889. Shady Cottage was the Fisher family's pioneer homestead, built in 1837 to replace the original log cabin on the site. It was a ten room, 3 storey stone house with a spacious verandah. It was reached by an avenue of maples and cedars, and was the centre of activity for the surrounding 200 acre farm. Shady Cottage was one of the first homes in town to be wired for electricity. The family had to put up their own poles along the Guelph Line from New Street. Homeowners along Guelph Line were allowed to take power from the new line, and were supposed to pay the Fisher family, although it was not always easy to collect! Burlington Mall now occupies the site of Shady Cottage and the farm.

When William took over the farm, it was a general farm with a large dairy herd which supplied much of the milk distributed in the Burlington area. However, in 1905, Fisher Farms entered the fruit growing market. The dairy herd was phased out, and the farm was planted with hickory nuts, mushrooms, raspberries, pears, plums, peaches, grapes and strawberries. Pears were each wrapped in paper for export to Britain. Good, old-fashioned apple varieties such as Talman Sweets, Spys and Baldwins were grown on the farm.

Every year, William wrote to Chief David Jack at the Six Nations Reserve and asked him to send down 30 or 40 fruit pickers. They remained on the farm for six weeks, picking strawberries and other small fruit. Strawberry pickers were paid one cent a box, and most could pick 300 to 500 boxes a day. Some stayed longer to work in the canning factories or to pick tree fruit. The Fishers were fond of their Indian friends. In their spare time, the Indians loved to play sports, and often made lacrosse sticks for the Fisher, and neighbouring, children. When Old Louis died on the farm, Indians came from all over to attend the funeral.

Farming families, like the Fishers and the Lindleys, who hired native people to work on their farms still feel that those people made a significant contribution to the development of farming in the Burlington area. On the whole, they were conscientious, dedicated people. Many became valuable employees who stayed with the same family for many years.

At one time, an Italian work train labourer, named Pedro, was ostracized for some reason by his fellow workers, and was thrown off the train near the Fisher farm. He asked for permission to sleep in the barn, and eventually moved into the house, doing general work. He was loved by all, and stayed for ten years. Eventually homesickness got the better of him, and William Fisher paid his passage back to Italy so that he could be reunited with his family.

In 1835, Peter Fisher had donated a piece of land as the site for a log school. It was the only school for miles around. In 1872, it was replaced by a brick school which remained until 1956. This school was "open concept" – one room for all grades. It boasted a rectangular stove that took 4-foot logs, a library of 100 books, and two cloak rooms (one for the boys, one for the girls). Since the well water on the school property tasted of sulphur, water was carried from the farm daily by two students. Students loved the huge white oak tree in the school yard, and used it as a centre for fun. It was the place to eat lunch, read a book, play games, or use as "home" for games of tag. Glenwood School, which replaced this school, was located on the southwest corner of Guelph Line and Glenwood School Drive. It was demolished in 1978.

Each September, the Burlington and Nelson Agricultural Society Fall Fair was held, and the Fishers always entered their fruit. At first, this fair was held on the Alderson farm on the Guelph Line just south of Highway 5. Later the event was moved to a large field on Brant Street between the Northwestern Railway and Graham's Lane. In 1925, the fairgrounds moved again to Queensway Drive on the present site of Barton Tubes Limited.

William Fisher was an organizer and president of the Ontario Fruit Growers Association. He also ran in two federal elections as the Liberal candidate.

For 20 years, William Fisher also farmed the land now known as Roseland Survey. He later sold it to Hughes Cleaver who developed it as a residential district.

William and Sarah's daughter, Edith who died in 1991, had many memories of growing up in Burlington. She remembered hearing that when her mother was a child on Elizabeth Street, the two churches — Trinity and Knox — were the centre of social life. When Sarah married William and went to live on the Guelph Line, she was bored living so far from town.

Edith and her friends often used to skate in winter by the water tower at John and Maria Streets. The water would overflow and freeze, making a good rink where many Burlington children learned to skate. As a young woman, she attended garden parties at W.D. Flatt's home on Lakeshore Road. Miss Fisher attended the Fisher school, and was often the only girl in the school. In her teens, she took the radial car to Hamilton to attend Central Collegiate, and afterwards went to the University of Toronto.

Fisher Farms are still in operation. Murray Fisher and his brother Paul added poultry to their operation and remained partners until 1949. During the Second World War, they purchased property on the north side of Highway 5, just west of the Guelph Line and when the Guelph Line property was sold for Burlington Mall, they moved their farming operation

...ob truck for feed mill, 1928.

—*Courtesy Rendell Job*

...he J. Rendell Job family. Front row — Walter Job, John Rendell Job, Ella Joan Easterbrook
...b. Back row — Annie Job, Thomas Easterbrook Job, Ethel Job Lambshead.

—*Courtesy Rendell Job*

there. Lumber from the old property helped to build the new one.

JOB, Walter

The name Job was well-known for many years, for the Job home stood on the corner of Job's Lane and Plains Road until 1990. Walter Job's parents settled on the farm on this site in 1893.

Walter continued the family's market garden operation, but in 1928 he also established a feed mill on Plains Road, representing Purina Chows. He was a pioneer in the feed business, becoming an expert on synthetic growth stimulants. For many years, he was the treasurer of the Ontario Feed Dealers Association. In 1950, he added broiler poultry to the small fruits and vegetables on his farm. Job's Lane and the Job home are gone, having been replaced by the Ikea development. Only the old Union Burial Grounds on the east side of the former Job's Lane reminds us that this was once a thriving pioneer community.

ROGERS, Joseph

Fate seems to have played a part in sending a good many fine families to Canada! When Joseph and Lavinia Rogers left England, they intended to go to Australia. However, when Lavinia saw the deplorable condition of the ship they were to sail on, she refused to go on board. The only other outbound ship was leaving for Canada, so the couple booked passage on it instead. The couple eventually reached Burlington, and in 1881 purchased Walton Home Farm from one of the Zimmermans. This farm was on Appleby Line at the top of the hill just south of the hamlet of Zimmerman.

Joseph Rogers Jr. married Mabel Wilkins, daughter of the postmaster. The couple lived at Walton Home Farm with his parents, and raised six children there. The children loved the apple orchard. They especially enjoyed the swing which hung from a special apple tree which bore large, sweet, light green fruit. For some reason, the children always pounded the apples to bruise them before eating them.

Among the village eccentrics at that time was Mrs. Johnson who always wore several bonnets, even when indoors. The miller, Mr. Bell, lived near the mill race in spite of the fact that he had lost a son to drowning there, and nearly lost a daughter in the same way.

THORPE, Edwin

When Edwin Thorpe settled in the Burlington area after emigrating from England, he first had a farm on Plains Road in Aldershot. Around 1887, however, he purchased a 35 acre farm at the corner of Maple Avenue and Fairview, the present site of Mapleview Mall. At first, Edwin built a small frame house on this property, where The Bay department store stands. In 1921, he enlarged the house and bricked it to create a gracious home.

Edwin's fruit trees, melons and tomatoes grew in abundance, for it was said that only two places in the world had better soil — the Nile delta and the Salinas Valley in California!

In the early 1930s, trucks began to replace fruit trains. Farmers liked this, because the truckers came to the farm to pick up produce, rather than the farmer having to take it to the railway station.

At that time, Burlington and Aldershot were famous for their cantaloupe, but eventually bacterial wilt proved to be their undoing. Now, a wilt-resistant melon can be grown successfully in the sandy soil of this area, but most of the former farm land has been taken over by development. In the opinion of Edwin Thorpe's grandson, Murray, it was the construction of the Queen Elizabeth Way through rural Burlington in 1939 which tolled the death knell of market gardening in this area.

In the late 1960s, Murray Thorpe and his brothers George and Allan sold the family farm to the developer, John Rosart. Other Maple Avenue farms purchased at the same time were owned by the Lindley family, Tregunno Brothers' seed company, the McCallums, the Bowens and the Robinsons. It took several years before Rosart Properties could get the zoning changed and services installed, but eventually the 130 acres north of Fairview Avenue were developed into Longos Fruit

Market and the Petro-Canada Plaza. South of Fairview, 453.6 acres were developed by Cambridge Shopping Centres into the 200 store Mapleview Mall which opened in September, 1990.

PEART, Ross

To a great extent, the success of market gardening in Burlington can be attributed to a descendant of an early pioneer farm family, Ross Peart. In addition to being a vegetable grower on Plains Road, Peart was first a fruit inspector. Later he installed heating plants in many of the greenhouses built in the late 1920s and early 1930s. He also became a dealer in pesticides and fertilizers, taking the trouble to study these products carefully and making special efforts to help farmers solve their problems as they arose.

Peter Lindley recalls that at one time, on his farm, he was experiencing difficulty with a molybdenum deficiency which causes whiptail in cauliflower. To compensate, molybdenum must be applied in a foliate spray. Ross Peart, then in his 80s, went directly to the supplier to get it, and brought it to the Lindley farm in Ancaster. On the way, he had an accident on Fiddler's Green Road at Highway 2, and it was devastating for Peter Lindley to see the Peart car in the ditch when he knew that its owner had been on the way to bring him the chemical needed to solve his problem. Ross Peart was not upset because the accident was not serious and he was glad to be helping a friend.

On another occasion, Peter Lindley found Ross Peart cleaning out a relative's barn with the help of Stan Claus. Since it looked like a big job, Peter Lindley pitched in to help. In the attic of the barn, he saw several small interesting stoves. When he admired one of them, Peart asked, "Where's your truck?" and insisted on loading the stove into it. The stove dated back to 1861, and had only been lit twice!

Ross Peart was revered by the farming community for his knowledge and common sense. When he was over 80, he was still trying new varieties of vegetables, and testing new practices, such as using plastic mulch for melons. His farm was

Ross Peart   *—Courtesy Murray Peart*

art farm on Plains Road. In foreground is Job Feed Mill. Across Job's Lane is the Pioneer metery. The Peart farm then extended to Q.E.W. and north to railway tracks. Now Ikea operty.

                                                       —Courtesy Murray Peart

on Plains Road adjacent to Union Cemetery. The house was demolished in 1990 to make way for highway expansion.

Ross Peart's great-grandfather had come from Weardale, England in 1817. He purchased land from Joseph Brant's widow, and later added to it so that he had extensive holdings. His son, Thomas, inherited the farm on the west side of the Guelph Line at the Queen Elizabeth Way. In turn, his only son, Arthur, later inherited the property which included the homestead known as The Maples. Arthur was interested in the science of fruit farming, and in 1896 he established the Burlington Experimental Station on his property, working closely with the Ontario Agricultural College and the Ontario Fruit Growers Association. As an expert in his field, Arthur Peart travelled extensively lecturing on fruit growing.

Arthur's son, Thomas Peart became a well-known medical doctor. He practised in Burlington from 1910 to 1929, then moved to Hamilton. He died of pneumonia at the age of 50.

Another member of the Peart family who accomplished a great deal in a short time was Harvey, son of Edwin Peart. After growing up on a farm in Nelson Township and graduating from the Ontario Agricultural College at Guelph, Harvey Peart was appointed director of the Horticultural Experimental Station at Vineland. The station was in very poor condition when he assumed the post. He was responsible for the planting of thousands of small trees and plants, and developed the station into a progressive centre which provided information for fruit growers all over the province. Harvey Peart, a diabetic, died at the age of 30.

BRADT, Albert

Having a home with a view must have meant a great deal to Albert Bradt, for in the last century, he traded a 200 acre farm in Caledonia plus $100 in cash for a hay farm on the hill at Lowville. The hill eventually became known locally as "Bradt's Mountain".

In the mid-19th century, Lowville was a busy village with a foundry, a furniture factory, a carpenter shop and a dressmaker. Miss Marsh's millinery shop later became George Bradt's harness shop, where he and his son worked at their trade until the early 1900s. By that time, the popularity of the automobile had resulted in a drastic reduction in their trade. George Bradt was well known locally for the fine honey he produced. Farm families liked to purchase a 25 lb. pail from him to last them through the winter. For many years, George Bradt's daughter, Mame, was organist at the Methodist church. This would not be notable, except for the fact that Mame came from a staunch Anglican family.

On the hill just north of Lowville was the settlement called Highville. Wooden steps were built up the hill to join the two communities in 1878, and later these steps were replaced by cement ones. Highville had its own post office, hotels, shops and, after 1907, the office of the Nelson Telephone Company. The shops included Culloden's general store, Miss Black's dressmaker shop, Klainka's tailor shop, and Pembroke's shoe shop. There was also the Emerson and McNair blacksmith and carriage shop.

HOPKINS, Silas

One of the earliest farming families in Nelson Township was the Hopkins family. When the land lottery was held in Nelson Township in 1806, Silas Hopkins drew the first ticket and was awarded Lot 3 on the north side of Highway 5 (Dundas Street). Three of his sons also farmed in the area. One of them, Ephraim, had property on the bay in Aldershot, as well as a farm at Dundas and Brant Streets.

At the turn of the century, W.J. Hopkins had an 80-acre farm called Bonnie Place. It boasted 15,000 apple, pear, peach and plum trees as well as currant bushes. The house, built in 1901, had hot running water and radiators, an innovation at the time. The main rooms of the house were finished in chestnut wood.

At the same time, William Van Norman Hopkins had a large farm on the Guelph Line, stretching from New Street to Prospect Street. In recent years, Esther Hopkins (a Hopkins married to a Hopkins) has reminisced about her life on this 100 acre farm. She remembers her father and a neighbour ploughing the Guelph Line after a snowstorm so that traffic could reach the lakeshore. She recalls the wonderful day in

1912 when electricity was turned on in their home for the first time. In 1915, relatives came from New York looking for the grave of Captain Silas Hopkins. They found it in a small family plot on the farm of his son, Gabriel, by the bay in Aldershot.

Perhaps it was William Van Norman Hopkins or his father (the family has many Williams) who in 1885 created a stir by refusing to pay the toll at the York Street entrance to Hamilton. Like other Halton and East Flamborough farmers, Hopkins was a "regular" at Hamilton market. To him and to other farmers, paying the toll added insult to injury, for it was a long and uncomfortable journey to take produce to the market over roads that were often next to impassable. Hopkins was brought before Wentworth County Judge John Sinclair who ruled in his favour. The proprietor of the toll gate company announced that he would continue to collect the tolls until the matter was decided by a higher court. The following day, Hopkins and about 20 other Burlington farmers forced their way past the gate on their way to market. By nightfall when the farmers were returning home, there was a clash with men hired to protect the gate as nearly 100 wagons charged through without paying. One farmer tried to pull the toll gate down with his wagon team. This sparked a general melee, and did nothing to alleviate the situation. There were more confrontations at the gate, and eventually it was torn down and tossed into the canal by a group of vigilantes. Even two years later, 15 farmers from East Flamborough and Nelson were charged $5 each plus $2 costs for charging past the toll gate without paying.

Both its beauty and its accessibility to Hamilton have made the city's western entrance very important. The Desjardins Canal was constructed to allow sailing vessels to reach Dundas which, in the early and mid 19th century, was a more important industrial centre than Hamilton. The original route of the canal was through Grindstone Creek, near the Valley Inn. However, in 1852, a channel was cut through Burlington Heights making the route shorter and straighter. A lower level swing bridge was built for the Great Western Railway line, while a wooden "high level" bridge was constructed to carry wheeled traffic. The toll gate was located just east of the Desjardins canal.

The first lower level bridge was destroyed in 1857 when a serious railway accident cost 60 lives and many injuries. At about the same time, the wooden high level bridge blew down in a severe storm. A new wooden bridge was built, but was soon condemned as unsafe, so farmers were then forced to use a lower level bridge built parallel to the railway bridge. This route was unpopular with the farmers, for it was difficult to negotiate with cumbersome farm wagons, and the horses were frequently frightened by passing trains. All of this, combined with the toll charge, created a great deal of dissatisfaction.

It wasn't until 1897 that a new iron high level bridge was built over the canal. Even then, the Hamilton and Milton Road Company continued to collect tolls, claiming that it had the right to do so until $60,000 in lost revenue from the lower level bridge was made up. Within two weeks of its opening, however, the toll was abandoned.

The present High Level Bridge replaced the iron one in 1931.

COLLING, Joseph

The name Colling is still closely associated with Lowville. Joseph Colling came from England in 1819, selected land on the Guelph Line on the hill south of Twelve Mile Creek, and returned to England to bring his family to their new home.

When the Nelson Circuit of the Methodist church was formed in 1832, Joseph Colling deeded one-eighteenth of an acre of his land, at the corner of Britannia Road and Guelph Line for a church. For many years, this was known as Colling Church. It is now Lowville United Church. Members of the Colling family are still associated with it.

There are many interesting stories associated with the church. At one time, when the Rev. Mr. D.B. Clappison was rector, there was no suitable house in Lowville for a manse, so one was rented in Kilbride. A fire threatened the parsonage, and neighbours pleaded with Mr. Clappison to leave the house. However, he remained on his knees praying. Finally, he rose to his feet and said, "Do not trouble yourselves, the parsonage will not burn." A moment later, the wind shifted, and the house was suddenly out of danger!

Even in the last century, citizens were protesting the encroachment of development on their peaceful domains. When residents of Lowville heard that the Credit Valley Railway might be going through the centre of their village, they demonstrated vigorously to local authorities. When it was announced that the railway would not go via Lowville, there was a huge celebration with a bonfire of stumps that had been saved up to build fences. Remember those stump fences, the farmer's way of recycling something that would otherwise be in his way?

In 1987, Florence Colling was still taking Burlington produce to Hamilton Market. She recalled the Depression years when she brought a crate of 36 pints of strawberries to market and couldn't even sell them for $1.75 for the whole crate. People just didn't have the money in those days. At that time, vendors on the market sold the produce they had grown themselves. Now, they are usually middle-men, selling what someone else has grown. People buy in smaller quantities now, too, because they don't have time for canning and can buy fresh produce all year round. Florence died in November, 1991.

MCCALLUM, Menzies

In the Maple Avenue neighbourhood, Menzies McCallum was "a different sort of a farmer". He didn't own any large farm equipment. In fact, he was hopeless when it came to mechanical things. Yet he had the greenest thumb of them all, and everything just seeemed to grow for him.

As a matter of fact, Menzies McCallum was ahead of his time, for he farmed with the environment, not against it. He could watch the clouds and test the wind, and tell just what sort of weather to expect. He didn't need to use a lot of scientific farming methods; he just farmed instinctively.

When he returned from World War II in 1945, he brought back Maud, an English war bride and raised a family of one son and four daughters. A true lover of Nature, Menzies owned a small piece of land-locked property at Hilton Falls, and loved to go there to fish. He and some of his friends used to go to a camp north of Algonquin Park to hunt every autumn. One year, while at the camp. he died of a heart attack.

A fitting end, his friends thought, for a man who loved and understood the out-of-doors.

BELL, Louis

Another well-known Maple Avenue fruit grower was Louis Bell. His grandparents, William and Edith Bell had purchased the family farm on Maple Avenue and Plains Road, across from the Lindleys, back in the 1850s.

Louis Bell and his neighbour, Ross Peart, shared a cultivating tractor which they bought jointly. This was an interesting alliance, for Louis was the opposite of Ross Peart. He was a good farmer, but very relaxed about it all. After a winter snowstorm, all his neighbours would be out busily shovelling snow away from their greenhouses. Louis would be sitting indoors, observing that "A Man up there brought it. He can take it away."

The Bell home was a popular refuge for local children who knew that cookies and candy were always offered when they visited there.

KEMP, Arthur

Some of the finest orchards in Ontario flourished in the Burlington area. Cherries, peaches, plums, apricots all grew abundantly. Some farmers, however, specialized in apples which seemed well suited to the soil. One of the well-known apple growers was Arthur Kemp whose 20 acre Strathcona Orchards were on Walker's Line. Arthur Kemp was born in Stoney Creek of parents who had emigrated from England. His father, who was employed as a market gardener, bought 10 acres on Guelph Line in 1925. He paid $1,000 an acre for the property which is now the site of Denningers, Canada Trust and the McDonald's restaurant.

As a boy, Art Kemp attended the one-room Fisher's Corners School at the junction of what is now the Q.E.W. and the Guelph Line. He recalls that in Grades 7 and 8, he was always first or second in the class; the only other pupil was Murray Pettit! When he graduated, he was given a bicycle

Two young St. John's Ambulance trainees receive proceeds of apple sales sponsored by Niagara Brand Chemicals from Art Kemp, President of the Ontario Fruit and Vegetable Grower Association around 1964.   —*Courtesy Art Kemp*

which he rode to Central High School in good weather. In inclement weather, he walked to the high school, cutting through Bell's Orchards on Brant Street.

While growing up, he worked with his three older brothers, Tom, Harold, and Hubert, and their father on the market garden land. Labour intensive crops such as spinach, radishes, lettuce, beets and carrots were grown early in the season, while they harvested cabbages, cauliflowers and staked tomatoes later in the growing year. During the Depression, the Kemps employed seasonal workers who often bicycled to the farm from Hamilton. They worked 59 hours a week, at 75 cents a day! The Kemp family said that they farmed 20 acres on their hands and knees. Tom was in charge of marketing. Six days a week in the growing season, he drove to the wholesale market in Toronto, arriving there at 5 a.m. with produce.

The original ten acres was gradually increased by the purchases of adjacent farm lands. One part of their holding at New Street and Guelph Line was later sold as the site of a Grand Union grocery store. It is now the location of the newly rebuilt Shoppers Drug Mart in Roseland Plaza.

After his marriage in 1940 to Isobel Smith, daughter of Lawrie Smith, Art worked for his father-in-law who was owner of Strathcona Orchards. On his return from service in the army during the Second World War, he went back to work at the orchards, and purchased this 200 acre property from Lawrie Smith in 1952.

After his leaving the army in 1946, Art Kemp joined the militia and became a lieutenant-colonel in the Lorne Scots Regiment, retiring in 1961. Mr. Kemp had many other interests as well. For four years, he represented the town of Burlington on the Inter-urban Area Board which was responsible for the maintenance of water services, and expanding these services to Nelson Township. He was also a member of the Burlington Fruit and Vegetable Growers Association, and for a year represented this group as a delegate to the Ontario Fruit and Vegetable Growers. In 1973, the provincial organization presented him with an award of merit for his many years of service as chairman of the apple section, and as president of the Ontario Fruit and Vegetable Growers.

Rose Josefik and mother, Josephine Novosad, picking tomatoes on Cumberland Avenue, 195
—Courtesy Frances Novosad Posave

Frank Novosad with his daughter Anne Novosad Kolar and baby Josephine.
—Courtesy Frances Novosad Posav

Art Kemp recalls that at one time, garden fertilizer did not come neatly packaged as it does to-day, but came from the Toronto stock yards in bulk lots. It was dropped off at the radial siding at New Street and Guelph Line where local growers picked it up. How times have changed at that intersection!

The original Guelph Line market garden farm known as Thomas Kemp and Sons is gone, too. Of the four Kemp brothers who came to that farm in 1925, Hubert and Art still live in Burlington, Harold died in 1959, and Tommy died in 1989.

Summing up his life, Arthur Kemp remarked that market gardening and fruit growing were not profitable businesses until the developers bought up the land!

NOVOSAD, Frank

Like many Czechoslovakian families, after the First World War, the Novosads lived for some years in Yugoslavia. In 1926, Frank Novosad left the town of Daruvar and came to Canada. At first, he worked as a carpenter in Hamilton. His wife Josefine and their two daughters joined him the next year. In the early 1930s, the Depression made it once again difficult for Frank to make a good living. He moved his family to New Street in Burlington where he worked on the market gardens. Later, he worked on the construction of the Bronte Bridge when the Queen Elizabeth Way was built.

When Mary Pettit began to subdivide her farm into five-acre lots, Frank Novosad decided to buy one. He paid $25 down on the $1,000 purchase price for the lot on the southwest corner of Cumberland Avenue and New Street. He built a two-roomed house, then cleared the brush and large trees from his property. On one occasion, when he dynamited a large stump, many snakes were rudely aroused from winter hibernation and thrown high into the air. Snakes were rarely seen in the neighbourhood after that!

Before long, lettuce, cauliflower, tomatoes and cabbages were planted, and greenhouses were built to start young plants. Often, the women carried on the market gardening operation while the men and older boys went to work at the large industries in Hamilton. Sometimes, the women also took

James and Frances Posavad with son Donny in 1945.   —*Courtesy Mary Sha*

seasonal work at the Glover Basket factory or Canadian Canners to supplement the family incomes. Frank's daughter, Frances, remembers that she went to work at Canadian Canners at the age of 12. A big girl, she was thought by her employer to be much older. During the busy season, she worked from 7 a.m. until 6 p.m., with one hour for lunch. She earned an average of $20 a week.

Other Czech families who settled on Cumberland Avenue farms were the Soukups, Selihars, Vihnaneks, Posavads and Surys. The families often got together for dances in their barns. Weddings, anniversaries, showers and other special occasions were celebrated with an abundance of food in someone's barn which would be white-washed inside and suitably decorated.

It was a close-knit community in which everyone worked hard, and took pride in their Czechoslovakian heritage. The families who settled on Cumberland Avenue as 20th century pioneers have made a great contribution not only to Burlington's agricultural community, but also to the city as a whole.

POSAVAD, James

The Posavads were another of the Czechoslovakian families who came to Burlington between the First and Second World Wars, and settled on small, five acre farms along Cumberland Avenue. It is a tribute to these families that Peter Lindley recalled in 1990 that his parents often took the children along Cumberland Avenue for a Sunday afternoon drive to admire the fine little farms there. "It says something about those people, that a family who had been farming in the area for 100 years went to see what the new people on the block were doing!"

The Posavads emigrated from Yugoslavia in 1938. At that time, each family was required to have $1,000 plus transportation costs. James and Frances Posavad and their four children arrived in Halifax with James' two brothers, Joseph and John, and their families. They travelled to Hamilton by train, and were met by friends from Vinemount. They might have settled at Vinemount, but their friend Frank Novosad convinced them that they should come to Burlington. The families purchased five-acre lots at $200 an acre from Mary Pettit who was newly widowed and was selling off parts of her farm.

James Posavad and his family spent the summer with the Novosads, sleeping in the garage while a house was being constructed on their land. Their daughter, Mary, worked for the summer on Hy Walker's farm, hoeing and picking fruit for ten cents an hour. In September, the children enrolled at the Fisher's Corners School. There was no road to the school from Cumberland Avenue at that time, so the children walked along the railway tracks to the Guelph Line. The teacher, Mary Lambshead, was very patient and understanding with these New Canadian children, and encouraged the other pupils to help them in every way possible.

Frances Posavad was anxious that her children should have fresh milk every day. They purchased a cow from Mrs. Pettit who allowed them to keep it in her barn. Morning and evening, Frances crossed the railway tracks to milk the cow which provided them with milk, cream and butter. The family also kept chickens, ducks and geese, not only for food, but also for the down for their feather beds. In the winter, the women had feather "bees", using only the finest down for their bedding.

It was the custom for the Czech families to marry among themselves. However, Mary Posavad broke this tradition when she married Bill Sharpe whom her father had met while working at Canadian Canners. During the Second World War, Bill was a cook with the R.C.A.F. His cooking skills won the hearts of Mary's relatives, and the couple was married in 1945. Mary and Bill's granddaughter, Lisa Sury, was Miss Teen Burlington in 1987, and was a runner-up in the Miss Teen Canada contest. Her parents are Bonnie and Karel Sury from another of the Cumberland Avenue pioneer families.

Mary Sharpe recalls that when the War began in 1939, Mary Lambshead taught the older girls at Fisher's Corners School to knit socks. One winter, Mary knit 25 pairs. Each knitter put her name on a slip of paper in the toe of the socks. To his astonishment, Bill Sharpe received a pair with Mary Lambshead's name in the toe!

BLESSINGER, Henry

Early Burlington, like its modern counterpart, was made up of a mix of ethnic groups. Henry Blessinger, for example, was of German descent. When he first came to Canada, he worked a rented farm in West Hamilton. He came to Aldershot in 1881 to settle on a 40 acre farm on the northwest side of Waterdown Road between the railway tracks and Plains Road. Henry and his wife, Maggie, had four children. The two older sons, Harry and Fred, had adjoining farms on Maple Avenue. Henry and his youngest son, Roy, ran the Aldershot farm, and in winter operated a coal business from the railway station on Waterdown Road.

The farm produced both fruit and vegetables. The Blessingers were the first in Aldershot to raise tomatoes in quantity. At that time, tomatoes were not popular with Hamilton consumers, so the Blessingers made three trips a week to the Guelph market. Henry, one of the first farmers to employ Indians from Brantford during the growing and harvesting seasons, provided wooden houses for them to live in on the farm.

Henry's two eldest sons, Harry and Fred, raised their families on Maple Avenue. The young people who wanted the advantage of a high school education had to attend school in Hamilton. Transportation was via the radial railway from the Brant Street station, and across the beach strip. During 1920-21, when the second half of the canal bridge was being constructed, passengers travelling to and from Burlington had to walk across a catwalk to the waiting radial car on the opposite side of the canal.

Henry's half-sister, Carolyn Fox, was the teacher at the little school on Howard Road. She resigned her teaching position to become the third wife of George Washington Johnson who was also a teacher, and who wrote the famous song "When You and I Were Young, Maggie" for his first wife, Maggie Clark.

In the fall of 1909, an epidemic of typhoid fever swept through Aldershot. Roy Blessinger was the first fatality. His daughter, Ruth, who was nine years old, also caught the disease, but recovered. Dr. John McGregor of Waterdown and

Blessinger family home on west side of Waterdown Road at Aldershot. —*Courtesy Elsie Ghe*

Fruit packing at Gallagher Farm, around 1920.   —*Courtesy Joseph Brant Museu*

his son, Dr. Ken McGregor, did their best to treat victims of the epidemic. The source of the disease was never found.

Henry and Maggie Blessinger sold the farm in 1910 and moved to a house at the corner of Locust and Birch Streets in Burlington. He died the following year, while Maggie lived until 1934. Of the Maple Avenue farms, Harry Blessinger sold his in 1920 and moved to Burlington to live near his parents. His farm was later owned by Murray Thorpe. Fred sold his farm to M.M. Robinson and also moved to Burlington. While they lived in Aldershot, all three Blessinger families were active at East Plains Methodist Church. At one time, there were five Blessinger girls in the choir.

GALLAGHER, John

The Gallagher family moved to the north side of Plains Road in 1879 when John Gallagher purchased 100 acres from the Fongers. At first, the Gallaghers carried on mixed farming with some livestock. Later, however, the fine fruit-growing soil encouraged John to plant fruit as well.

In 1910, John's son George took over the family farm. About ten years later, George acquired the adjoining 65 acre farm, owned by Robert Johnson. Forming a partnership with his four sons — Howard, Gordon, Percy and Norman — he phased out the livestock operation and grew fruit only under the name of Gallagher Farms. The family used the registered trade mark Sunfruit for their apples, and their famous "Sugar-Salmon" cantaloupes. The Gallaghers discovered this variety of cantaloupe as a natural cross between the early green-fleshed "Sugar-Sweet" variety grown locally and a late variety with the desirable salmon colour. Realizing the value of an early salmon flesh melon, they saved the seed and planted it the following year, with the result that about a third of the fruit was salmon in colour. Seed from these melons was saved and planted the following year. After the fourth year, the melons were all salmon-fleshed, and every grower in Aldershot was anxious to switch to "Sugar-Salmon" for the early crop.

Also grown on the farm were 2,250 apple trees of such popular varieties as Delicious, McIntosh, Red Spy and Court-

SUNFRUIT

TRADE MARK REG.

BRAND

DEPENDABLE

APPLES

are famous for their

Fine Flavor

and

Excellent
Keeping Qualities.

Grown and Packed by

GALLAGHER FARMS

Label of Sunfruit Brand Apples.
—*Courtesy Joseph Brant Museum*

Fruit Growers Field Day at Gallagher Farm in 1927.　　　—*Courtesy Joseph Brant Museum*

land. Some of the Northern Spy and Greening trees which John planted in 1882 continued to bear fruit until 1965 when Gallagher Farms ceased to exist. The farm also grew tart cherries, grapes and strawberries.

George Gallagher's wife, Annie Whatmough, was a native of Toronto. Her father was a staunch Methodist who would not enter any other church. When visiting his daughter and her family, he went to East Plains Church while they attended the service at St. Matthew's Anglican Church. The Gallaghers were strong supporters of this little church. Six generations of this pioneer family attended Sunday School there.

When George and Annie's son, Howard, was presented with an agricultural service diploma from the Flamborough and Waterdown Agricultural Society in 1952, the event was celebrated at the family farm. Nearly 100 guests met at the farm pond which provided the water for spraying the fruit trees. The tour continued on to the orchards and the cold storage shed, finishing at Mrs. Gallagher's workshop where she produced ceramics made from the clay of the pond.

Ann Gallagher — sister of Howard, Gordon, Percy and Norman — was a noted artisan who produced unusually beautiful blown glass plates and other pieces with bubbles within the glass. Her studio was in the old Gallagher home. Some of her works were displayed in corporate offices in Hamilton.

Gordon Gallagher was very active in both country and town affairs. He was on the town planning committee which drew up the first Official Plan, one of the first in Ontario. He was on the provincial Good Roads Committee, and served as both deputy reeve and reeve of Burlington. He was also an active member of the Burlington Historical Society and held the office of president.

The Gallagher home, built by John in the early 1880s, is still standing at the corner of Plains Road East and Gallagher Road, and is still occupied by descendants of John Gallagher.

John Gallagher's eldest son, Richard Edward, grew up on the farm but chose a career in business. He attended Canada Business College in Hamilton, and later purchased the college when the owner wished to retire. Mr. Gallagher successfully operated the school from 1880 to 1932, winning the respect and admiration of the students. For his textbook on commercial law and his other contributions to business education, he was given the honorary title Doctor of Laws by the Nashville College at Nashville, Tennessee.

His son, Herbert, also chose a business career. After moving to California, he became an organizer of the Shell Oil Company of California, and was the company's first vice-president, general manager and director.

BRECKON, W.E.

There was a great deal of jubilation in Burlington in 1954, especially in the farming community. That was the year that W.E. Breckon became the World Wheat King, and was honoured with a dinner and presentation ceremony at Fairview School in Lowville.

Bill Breckon's grandparents came from England in 1830, and settled on a 100 acre grant of land on the north side of Middle Road (the Queen Elizabeth Way) just west of what is now Burloak Drive. When their grandson took over the farm in 1921, he purchased an adjoining 63 acres, and, in 1933, added 33 acres on the northwest corner of the Q.E.W. and Burloak Drive. In the 1940s, he added another 150, thus giving him a total of 350 acres.

At first, the farm maintained a dairy herd of about 40 head of Jersey cattle. Milking was done by hand in the morning and in the evening, seven days a week, with the milk picked up each morning by dairies in Burlington and Toronto. The Breckons also did some mixed farming, but later put in extensive crops of grain. In the early 1940s, W.E. Breckon was a director of the Halton Crop Improvement Association and the Ontario Crop Improvement Association, groups formed by the Ontario Department of Agriculture to help farmers improve their crop yields. It was learned that Cornell University in New York State had developed a superior winter wheat called Genesee. The O.C.I.A. asked if they could have a small quantity of this wheat to be used by Ontario farmers. Cornell University complied, sending 30 bushels. W.E. Breckon was one of 15 farmers to try the wheat.

Mr. W. E. Breckon.

For some time, Bill Breckon had noticed that the clay soil on his farm seemed to have some special property that produced very white wheat. On one occasion, he sold some wheat to a Milton farmer, and the next year bought some of the seed back to finish sowing a field. Although it was seed from his own wheat, it showed as a dark streak in his field as the crop grew. He never did discover the nature of that special quality in his farm's soil.

For nine consecutive years, Mr. Breckon entered his wheat in the white winter wheat class at the Royal Winter Fair. In his first eight tries, he won seven Firsts and a Second. Then, in 1954, his entry of Genesee winter wheat won not only first prize in its category but also the overall World Wheat Championship, competing against the first prize winners in each of five categories. Breckon wheat won over entries from all over the world. It was the first time the championship had been won by a grower from eastern Canada. The prize consisted of a cheque for $100 and a silver tray.

Bill Breckon's wife, the former Susie Atkinson, played an important part in the farm operation. She hand-picked the specimens of wheat which were entered in the competitions at the Royal Winter Fair.

W.E. Breckon was impressed by the publicity his achievement received. When he was invited to Cornell University, the customs officer at Fort Erie asked, "Are you that farmer from Ontario who won the wheat championship?" He was especially proud of a letter he received from a Manitoba farmer. It read simply: "Hi, Bill. Doggone it, we're proud of you!" The letter is now at the Ontario Agricultural Museum in Milton.

In 1957, Burlington council passed a motion to annex the southern part of Nelson Township to Highway 5, and to include the properties to the north facing Highway 5. A public meeting was held at 10 a.m., and Mr. Breckon asked if he could be the first speaker, since he had to attend a meeting in Toronto. He pointed out that, as a school board member, he felt that both Burlington and Nelson would be better served under amalgamation because one school board would be more efficient than the three that existed (Burlington and Nelson public school boards and Burlington high school board). He learned later that at a special meeting held during the lunch break, Burlington council rescinded its original motion and passed another one taking in all of Nelson. Not only was this approved at the public meeting, but also part of East Flamborough and Aldershot asked to be included in the annexation as they could obtain Burlington water more cheaply than from Hamilton. Consequently, Burlington became many times larger, almost overnight.

Mr. Breckon is remembered for his accomplishment as World Wheat King, and for his many years of devoted service on the school board, in the name of W.E. Breckon School on Tuck Drive. When the Breckon family had a reunion at Bronte Creek Park (site of the original family farm) in 1984, the Wheat King was the oldest family member in attendance.

As one of the early families to arrive in the Burlington area, the Breckons have intermarried with many other pioneer families. When George Bell was born in 1909, his arrival created a five-generation family on his mother's side. This included Mrs. John Breckon of Appleby who was his great-great-grandmother; Mrs. John Ryan, his great-grandmother; Mrs. A. Alton, his grandmother; and Mrs. William Bell, his mother. All told, George had six grandmothers and five grandfathers living!

ALTON, George

The Altons, along with the Breckons, were among a group of families who emigrated from the village of Appleby in Westmoreland, England, and established the settlement of Appleby in Halton. These families have been closely associated ever since. When Dudley Lucas Alton married Olive Christina Breckon in 1917, it was the third time that the two families had been joined in matrimony. Mary Ann Breckon had married David Alton in 1854, and the two had a family of 13 children. Captain John Breckon married Sara Ann Alton in 1869, and raised seven children.

The Altons were farmers, and it was a hard life at times. Often, they turned to other enterprises to add to the family income and provide an extra challenge to life. For example, much of the brick for the first houses in Appleby was made from the excellent red clay found on Daniel Alton's farm.

George Havelock Alton told his son, Dudley, that he had ruined his health as a young man by the heavy work he had done. He helped his father who had taken the contract to make the approaches to the new bridge over Twelve Mile Creek at Highway No. 5. This required widening the steep bank to accomodate the road, and the work was all done by hand. There was no earth-moving equipment in those days! It took all summer to complete the job. George's reward was a silver hunter's-case pocket watch which is still treasured by the Alton family.

George Havelock Alton was born in 1867 on the original George Shepherd Alton farm on Dundas Street at the corner of Walker's Line. His father was the first generation of the Altons to be born in Canada, and his mother was Margaret Cline, a descendant of John Cline who had come to Canada from the United States about 1803. George was a natural mechanic, and could repair any kind of machine or engine. He bought a steam engine and a saw mill, and equipped his own blacksmith shop so that he could repair his own and his neighbours' machinery. Always thinking of how to develop laboursaving devices, he attached a gasoline engine to the washing machine, and to a saw that cut the stove wood.

Many Alton descendants inherited mechanical skills. For years, Alton's garage located on Highway 5 at Walker's Line and owned by Colin Alton and his sons, serviced cars, trucks and tractors for local residents as well as highway travellers.

In 1891, George Havelock Alton married a member of another pioneer Burlington family, May Victoria Lucas. She, too, was an interesting person. Named after the Queen of England, she was usually called Birdie. After her marriage to George Alton, she and her husband took over her family's farm because her father had been killed when he was thrown from his rig on the road down to the Twelve Mile Creek bridge. Like other women of her day, she was a capable housewife, raising chickens, and selling butter and eggs to the grocers in Burlington. She kept a bcx of herbal remedies so that she could treat her family's minor illnesses. Her favourite treatment was

ʀuce & Bob Alton, sons of Colin, owner of Alton's Garage on #5 Highway, between 1933-1988.
—*Courtesy Douglas Alton*

ᴅavidson Nurseries.   —*Courtesy Phyllis Brandon*

rhubarb root for constipation, much to the discomfort and chagrin of her patients! Dr. Anson Buck who practised in Palermo treated more serious problems.

George and May's daughter, Nora, became a school teacher. She married her cousin, Harold Burkholder, and they moved to western Canada where they tried gold mining for a while. Later, they returned to Ontario. When her father died in 1942, Nora and her family moved to the farm to live with her mother. Eventually, the farm was sold to the government where it became part of Bronte Creek Provincial Park.

DAVIDSON, Charles

As so often happened in small towns like Burlington, Minnie Allen, daughter of carriage-maker James Allen, married a village boy, Charles Davidson, of another well-known local family. John and Hannah Davidson had come from Northumberland, England in 1830, and purchased 100 acres on Walker's Line from Thomas Foster. In the mid-1800s, their son, John, operated a nursery on Guelph Line. He was probably the first nurseryman in Nelson. His home was on the west side of the road, while the farm was on the east side. When the Maple Avenue swamp was drained, he and his wife, Jane, bought property on Lockhart Road at Maple Avenue and moved the nursery to that location. This was where the family lived when John and Jane's son, Charles, married Minnie Allen in 1885. Charles took the business over in 1902.

In the same year, Charles and Minnie's daughter, Constance, was born. She began her education at the age of seven when she went to the one-roomed school on Plains Road at Maple Avenue. Her teacher was Helen Pattinson who, she felt, paid more attention to the pupils of Junior Fourth and Senior Fourth (Grades 7 and 8) than she did to the younger students. Con, as she was called, attended Burlington Central Continuation School briefly, then commuted to Hamilton by radial car to attend Central Collegiate. After matriculating, she took a general degree at Victoria College at the University of Toronto, graduating in 1925.

At her father's request, after graduation she returned home to help with the nursery business. Maple Avenue market

lan Davidson taking fruit to Freeman Station.　　　　　—*Courtesy Phyllis Brandon*

laud (Mrs. W. J. Cannom), Fred, Ina (Mrs. Joseph Lambshead), Hannah Davis (Mrs. Thaddeus hent), Thaddeus Ghent, Lucy (Mrs. B. O'Dell).　　　　—*Courtesy Margaret O'Dell*

gardeners recognized and respected Con's "green thumb". Later, she married Cecil Danielsen, born in England of Danish descent. At the time of writing, she lives in the upper duplex of a Maple Avenue home built by her brother, Allan Davidson, in 1931.

Four generations of Davidsons carried on the nursery business on Lockhart Road. After Charles, his son-in-law, Cecil Danielsen, operated the business. Cecil's son, Allan, was not interested in the nursery business, and went into the wholesale fruit business instead. However, his son, David, graduated from the University of Guelph and went into the family greenhouse business.

David's sister, Phyllis, recalled recently that in spring, quantities of roses and fruit trees were purchased for re-sale. Each rose bush had to be dipped into melted paraffin wax. The children liked to dip their hands into the wax and let it harden. Tomatoes and cucumbers were grown in the greenhouses also.

When David operated the business, he branched out into bedding plants such as geraniums and marigolds. Seedlings were shipped to cities across Canada. Also, trees from Davidson's nursery were sold to the Metropolitan Toronto Parks Board to provide shade in city parks. David is now a salesman for Stokes Seeds.

In the Joseph Brant Museum, there is a picture of the old wharf at the foot of Brant Street showing Mrs. Danielsen's father, Charles Davidson, packing apples to be sent abroad.

GHENT, Thomas

One of the first families to settle in Brant's Block was the Ghents. They had originally come to North America from Wales, settling in Maryland, then moving to North Carolina. As sympathizers with the British during the American Revolution, they were severely persecuted.

Thomas Ghent (or Gant, as the name was then spelled) came to Canada with his wife's family, the Davises, and was one of the early settlers in Saltfleet Township. In true pioneering spirit, he purchased land from Joseph Brant in 1804, and moved his family once again, this time to become one of

eeman General Store & Post Office, owner W. J. Cannom at lower right — married Maud
hent.

—Courtesy Frank Armstrong

James Vyse, with the Fairfield School on left.

—Courtesy Stan Wickens

the founding families at Wellington Square. For 150 years, members of the Ghent family farmed continuously in Burlington.

In 1902, William Ghent owned an extensive farm on the west side of Brant Street between the village of Burlington and the Grand Trunk Railway station at Freeman. His nine room brick home was known as Maple Lodge. In one year, the farm produced 10,000 quarts of strawberries, 3,000 quarts of raspberries, 36 tons of tomatoes, 90 tons of mangolds (a turnip-like vegetable used for cattle fodder), 2,000 crates of melons, 12 tons of cabbages, eggplant and peppers. The extensive orchards were planted with apple, pear, plum, cherry and peach trees. The farm also produced wheat, barley and oats with a yield of 53 bushels per acre.

This was one of the farms on which it is said that William Lyon Mackenzie took refuge in 1837 when fleeing after the rebellious confrontation at Montgomery's Tavern in Toronto. In 1902, the property was advertised for sale for $10,000. Ghent Avenue is named after this pioneer family.

WICKENS, George

George Wickens worked for the Spratt Pet Food Company in England, but when he immigrated to Canada, he began an entirely different life as a market gardener. George and his wife, Minnie, arrived in Aldershot in 1921 with their young sons, Sydney and Frank. Their eldest son, Roland, had already settled in this area.

George and Minnie purchased a four acre farm on Plains Road, next to Inverness which was then the Easterbrook home. The farm was later inherited by Frank who continued to farm while holding a second job in the insurance business. Sydney attended Park Business College in Hamilton, then opened a grocery store. When this failed during the Depression, he returned to Aldershot to work on the farm of a family friend, George Atkins. In time, he was employed by Imperial Oil and remained with this company until his retirement. The family lived on Waterdown Road, overlooking J. Cooke's cement plant.

LEMON, William

Just west of Hidden Valley Road and Grindstone Creek in Aldershot is Lemonville Road. It is named after the Lemon family who were well-known in the Aldershot farming community for many years.

William Lemon was born in Lynden, where he farmed for many years. Around the turn of the century, he moved to Plains Road, and became engaged in fruit farming. When he retired in 1917, he moved to the house at 85 Martha Street in Burlington. There are still Lemons living in Aldershot.

ALMAS, James

When Christopher Almas was a young man in Prussia, he was conscripted into the army, and served with the Hessian troops who fought with the British during the American Revolution. After the war, he remained in the United States, and married Magdalena Baker who had four children. They had been badly treated by the Americans, so in 1797, they came to Canada and settled in Ancaster. Christian Almas, as he was now known, owned 166 acres on the southwest corner of what is now Mohawk Road West and Paradise Road. This property passed down to his great-great-grandson before finally being developed as part of Hamilton. As the Almases all had large families, Christian and Magdalena had many descendants.

Early in this century, James Almas decided to move to Burlington.

He married Mary Jane Lambshead, and farmed a large tract of land on Maple Avenue. Members of this large, close family frequently travelled back and forth across the York road to visit each other. When James died, his property was divided equally among his sons, Gordon, Fred, Ernie, Clayton and Ross. Clayton had suffered from measles when he was 18 months old. Many other local children were stricken in the same epidemic, and several had died. Clayton was left with a mental disability, so one of his brothers farmed his portion of the property on his behalf.

Ernie's family was also dogged by tragedy. In 1939, Ernie died intestate, leaving his wife, Nellie, with five children. In

Almas & Sons, Freeman, with Great Grandpa Lambshead. —*Courtesy Lillian Ruth Simm*

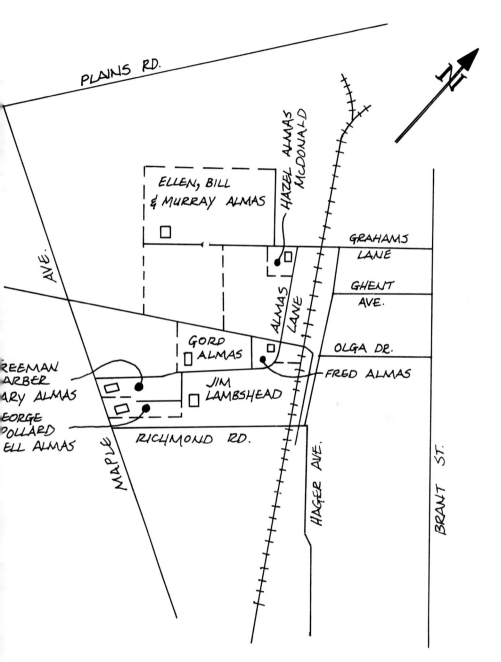

lmas farms at Plains Road & Maple Ave. —*Courtesy Lillian Ruth Simmons*

the tradition of rural society, neighbours pitched in to help with the farm. A year or so later, the family suffered again when a teen-aged son, Jim, died of a malignant melanoma. In 1951, the youngest daughter, Muriel, who was then in her early 20s, died suddenly of a viral infection. In spite of this, Nellie continued to farm on Maple Avenue, and was respected by her neighbours as a good farmer. Her son, Bill, is still farming at Troy, Ontario.

Ross, James and Mary Jane's youngest son, decided to go into the ministry, and sold his share of the family farm to his brother, Fred. He hoped to go to South Africa as a missionary for the Associated Gospel Churches of Canada, but due to lack of funds and his health problem, the Church was not able to send him. Instead, Ross spent 18 years as a circuit preacher at Corson's Siding, a lumber town near Coboconk.

Ross's son, Paul, still remembers the culture shock of coming to Burlington after living at Corson's Siding for all of his young life. After attending a one-room school with a handful of other students, he was overwhelmed on his first day at East End School (now Lakeshore School). However, he soon settled in, and enjoyed walking all the way across town with his friends to jump into the swimming hole at the foot of Nelson Avenue. For a young lad, he recalls, crossing Brant Street was like going into a different world. Later, when he attended Glenwood School, he remembers looking across the road at the rows of vineyards.

His sister, Ruth Simmons, has vivid memories of Graham's Lane which ran through the northern portion of the Almas farms. Called Cinder Lane by the locals because it was coated with cinders from the railway trains nearby, the path was dark and tunnelled with bushes. The children found it very "spooky", and often ran through there as fast as they could on their way home from Sunday School at the Freeman Gospel Chapel on Brant Street. A tractor path, known as Almas Lane, ran through the Almas farms from Graham's Lane to Maple Avenue. *see map.

SMITH, J.C.

Maxwell Smith was not the only member of his family to be a notable figure around Burlington. His father, John Chamberlain Smith, a respected fruit grower, was often called Apple Jack. John and his wife, Sarah Boothman, raised a family of four sons and four daughters – Maxwell, Grant, Wallace, Frank, Ethel, Irene, Maud and Marian. The first three sons followed their father into the fruit business. The fourth, Frank, became a mining engineer. Marian died at the age of three of diphtheria. Maud always lived at home.

At first, the family lived on the north side of Water St. near the Gore, and it was here that the children were born. When Frank, the youngest, was five years old, they moved to Apple Villa on the northeast corner of Lakeshore Road and Smith Avenue. The 20 acre farm extended up to New Street. The stately brick home was purchased from William Dalton. To-day, it is distinguished by the red, green and white shutters which were painted in this manner when the house was used as a consulate for the Netherlands.

Every year, Mr. and Mrs. Smith travelled to Nova Scotia to arrange the sale of the McIntosh apples and Bartlett pears which they grew on their farm. Some of their produce was shipped overseas by boat, a daring venture in those days before reliable refrigeration.

Mrs. Smith was a fine-looking lady. One morning, she came downstairs and announced that that was the day she would die. She had dreamed of herself in a casket, wearing her wedding dress. She did die that day, sitting quietly at the table.

Maxwell Smith bought the house across the road from his parents' home in 1905. It is now Brant's Landing. His career as a business man and politician is described elsewhere in this book.

Grant Smith travelled through the West buying apples, and ended up in the Yukon with his brother Frank and sister-in-law Floss. Wallace was a fruit jobber who at one time worked for his father in South Africa.

Frank's wife, Flossie, met the Smith family when she was a student nurse at Hamilton's St. Joseph's Hospital. She was

Home of J. C. Smith, corner of Smith Ave. and Lakeshore Rd.
—*Courtesy Mrs. F. L. Smith*

The Smith Family, 1954. Ruth (daughter of Wallace), Wallace, Grant, Maud, Margaret (wife
of Grant), Jack (son of Wallace), Irene, Aileen (wife of Wallace), Frank, Floss (wife of Frank).
Maxwell is missing.   —*Courtesy Mrs. F. L. Smith*

sent to look after Maud who had broken her leg. During her recuperation, Maud told Flossie many stories about the family. For example, one foggy night, J.C. Smith came in and said, "Somebody's going to be killed at Rambo Creek." So he took a pail of whitewash and painted the edges of the road around the curve, and a line down the middle. Perhaps this inspired Maxwell Smith to think of the white line for the newly constructed Lakeshore Highway in 1914!

IRELAND, Joseph

In May, 1991, the City of Burlington proudly opened its second museum — the Ireland House on Guelph Line just north of Upper Middle Road. Known as Oakridge Farm because of its location on a rise in the land, the house was built between 1835 and 1837 by Joseph Ireland. Until recently, the house was occupied by his descendants. It is a gem for the city because it still contains the original furnishings.

Joseph Ireland's youngest son, John, inherited the farm from his father in 1869. His eldest son, Robert, inherited three large farms nearby which Joseph had acquired over the years. When John died in 1904, there were still eight of his 12 children living at home on the farm. Part of the property was sold in 1905, leaving about 130 acres including a large area of bush.

The Irelands carried on mixed farming. They had a herd of cows, and grew grain and corn for the feed. There were also orchards of apples which were shipped overseas, as well as cherry, pear and plum trees for the family's own use. One of the plums cultivated on the farm was registered as the "Ireland seedling." The farm also grew black and red currants, straw-berries and a variety of vegetables.

Like other farmers of the day, the Irelands kept a few pigs and chickens for their own table. For several years, they made butter, and delivered it as well as eggs to Hamilton homes, including Dundurn Castle.

The family was a close one, with the older girls looking after the younger boys. The boys loved to torment their sisters in their courting days. When one of the girls became engaged, she was allowed to entertain her fiance in the parlor with the

Nelson Women's Institute at Ireland House around 1910. Back row — Margaret Wilson, Cla
Mitchell, Mrs. F. Featherstone, President, Mrs. J. B. Alton, Mrs. Arthur Freeman, Mrs. J.
Griffin, Mrs. Sam Sinclair and Jonathan, Lucy Springer (Mrs. George Ireland), Daisy All
(Mrs. Charles Ireland), Mrs. Edwin Peart, Miss Maud Ireland, hostess. Front — Mrs. Jol
Emerson, Ethel Alton, Chrissie Wilson, Muriel Peart, Ethel Emerson, Kathleen Peart.
—Courtesy Nelson Women's Institu

Limestone Farm Forum, around 1955. This photo includes the Watsons, Readhea
Richardsons, and Collings. *—Courtesy Irma Coulson & Canadian Champi*

door closed. In the hall, there is a stove built into the wall so that it heated the parlor and the adjacent room. In warm weather, the boys crawled into the stove to listen to the couples' conversations. In cold weather, these same boys stoked the fire so fiercely that the overheated couple was forced to open the door! Visitors to the Ireland House can see that stove to-day.

The family was active in the life of St. John's Anglican Church on Highway 5, the parish which Joseph Ireland helped to found. The girls were Sunday School teachers and sang in the choir, while one was the organist. Another sister was a founding member of the Nelson Women's Institute.

Most of the Irelands loved to dance, and attended many of the regular dances held at Nelson, Appleby, Palermo and Milton. Often, they would dance the night away, and arrive home by buggy in time to change clothes and start the work of the day.

George Ireland was the last of John's children to remain at home. Since he was anxious to farm, he bought out his brothers' and sisters' shares in the property. He continued to farm until the 1960s, when the property was sold to developers, except for the house and about four acres of land. George's only child, Marie, lived there until her death in 1985.

The City of Burlington bought the house in 1987, with all of its artifacts and furnishings donated by Helen Ireland Caldwell. Now, Burlingtonians and visitors to the city can journey briefly into the past through a tour of Oakridge Farm.

Fruit in Glover baskets waiting for the fruit train.   —*Courtesy National Archives of Canada*

The Bridge Club on a weekend up north: Ruth and John Blair, et al.
                    —*Courtesy Helen Lindley Langford*

II

BUSINESSMEN

Among the most important people in the community were those who perceived a need, and went about filling it. The early businessmen in Burlington were often part-time farmers, since their town was still basically a rural one. Yet once they observed the need for a particular product – such as fruit baskets or specialized merchandise – they were quick to plunge into new ventures that often proved to be both successful and profitable.

As Burlington's needs have changed over the years, so have the businesses and the people behind them. Many names from the past are still familiar in modern Burlington, and the legacy of service to the public remains.

GLOVER, W.T.

As the lumber industry waned and fruit growing expanded, a new need developed in the Burlington area. Suddenly, there was a demand for baskets in which to pack the abundant produce.

W.T. Glover was a successful fruit grower, but he could see that there was money to be made in the basket industry as well. In 1893, he formed the Burlington Box, Barrel and Basket Works at Freeman. Huge numbers of elm and basswood logs were brought to the factory to be turned into fruit containers, including the imperial crate which Glover had developed himself.

In 1908, the name of the firm became W.T. Glover Manufacturing Co. Ltd. By this time, Glover baskets were being shipped from coast to coast. Later, the company was absorbed by Oakville Wood Specialties Ltd. which is still in operation, although not in Burlington.

Burlington had another basket factory as well — Dalton's, located at the corner of Nelson Avenue and Lakeshore Road, where the Burlington Cultural Centre stands now. The Fosters on Blind Line sold their woodlot to Dalton's in the early 1900s. During the winter, farmers hauled logs from the Foster farm to the factory.

Since they contain so much flammable material, basket factories have a high incidence of serious fires. Dalton's burned in 1914, and the Glover basket factory burned in 1966. Neither was rebuilt. This was not the first time that the Glover company had suffered from fire. A newspaper clipping dated 1937, describes another Glover fire as "one of the biggest fires in the town for a number of years." At that time, Glover was renting storage space from the Burlington Co-operative Fruit and Vegetable Growers Association at Freeman, and had the building completely packed with baskets. The fire was so fierce that it could be seen for miles around. The railway station, which had just been painted, was badly blistered, and boxcars on the tracks were too hot to touch. The loss to the Co-op was $8,000, while Glovers lost $10,000. Both sums were partially covered by insurance, but a local farmer, A.E. Rusby who had seed potatoes stored in the basement was not insured.

BLAIR, George

Some things have not changed much. A hundred years ago, many farmers had other skills and other jobs in addition to farming. One of these was George Blair who was first a carpenter in Kilbride. A widower, in 1893 he married the widowed Hannah Shephard. They began their married life with five children from their first marriages. This required a spacious home, so they moved to the Nelson Ogg farm on Brant Street. The farm extended to George Street on the east, and to Ghent Avenue on the north. The house, Blairholm, is still standing at the corner of Brant Street and Blairholm Avenue. On June 20th, 1990, George's eldest son, Stanley Blair, celebrated his 100th birthday in this house.

For many years, the Blairs grew fine Spy apples on the 50 acre farm. Some of these were sold locally, and until the First World War broke out, others were shipped to Scotland

and England. The farm also produced potatoes, asparagus, watermelon and strawberries.

But George Blair was not only a farmer. His background in carpentry led him to build many fine homes during the 1880s. For example, on Burlington Avenue, he built number 419 for George Knife, a painter and wood grainer, and number 432 for Mr. Grier who was a Toronto accountant. Blair himself lived at 472 Burlington Avenue until he moved "out of town" to the Ogg farm at the time of his second marriage. The house at 482 Burlington Avenue, known as Maplelawn, was built by Blair for the widow of a lawyer named Gordon.

George Blair also built the house at 468 Locust Street for Robert Kentner who had a farm on Plains Road in Aldershot. When his sons, John and Stanley, took over the family farm, Blair built a home for John and his bride, Ruth Breckon, at 701 Brant Street. Many of these fine old homes feature beautifully carved curving staircases for which George Blair was well known.

George Blair's son, John, played an active part in town affairs, serving on town council in the 1930s, then becoming deputy reeve and reeve. He and his wife were founding members of the Burlington Historical Society.

During the early 1900s when the Blair children were growing up, Burlington was still a rural community. The Gazette cost $1 a year. Oil lamps on Brant Street had just been replaced by electric street lights. Population was 1,200. By 1936, the population had grown to 3,560.

After the Second World War, things changed dramatically. Farms all over Burlington were being subdivided for housing. George and Hannah Blair's children hung on as long as they could, but by 1955, the handwriting was on the wall. The Blair farm was subdivided, and Brant Street lost its rural ambience forever.

The Blair name remains, however, enshrined in street names, and in the lovely homes built by George Blair so long ago.

HENDRIE, William

William Hendrie came to Canada in 1855 to take a position with the Great Western Railway in Hamilton. He had not been with the railway long before he noticed some inefficiencies in the freight delivery system. Although only 24 years old, he left his position to form a partnership with John Shedden to act as cartage agents for the railway. The partnership only lasted three years, but Hendrie's contracts with the Great Western and many other railways turned him into a very wealthy man.

Hendrie's main residence was "Holmstead" on Bold Street in Hamilton. However, he also owned the 122 acre Valley Farm at the western extremity of Aldershot. Hendrie first raised Holstein cattle on the farm, as well as Leicester and Cotswold sheep. Later, he raised purebred race horses, at one time having 300 on his farm. In this, he was as successful as in his other business enterprises. One of his horses, Martinmas, won a total of $52,000 during his lifetime. In fact, his winnings in the Futurity Stakes were donated to the Hamilton General Hospital to finance the building of a wing.

The Hendrie farm had a half-mile practice race track at Unsworth Avenue. There was also a stable for retired cartage horses from the C.N.R. in Hamilton. Part of the farm was surveyed for lots in 1922.

William Hendrie was one of the original organizers and shareholders of the Ontario Jockey Club, and an honorary member of the English jockey club. However, he consistently opposed race-track betting. He was also one of the organizers of the Hamilton Great Central Fair, and at one time was president of this event.

William's eldest son, Sir John S. Hendrie, graduated from Upper Canada College in Toronto, then worked as a civil engineer with several railways in Ontario. He then joined the Hamilton Bridge Works which had been founded by his father. He served first as manager and vice-president, then as president. In 1901 and 1902, he was mayor of Hamilton, and in 1914 he was appointed lieutenant-governor of Ontario. Sir John maintained Valley Farm, and with his brother, George, had an extensive racing stable which won the King's Plate on two occasions.

The second Hendrie son, William, also had an outstanding career as president and manager of Hendrie and Company Limited, Grand Trunk Railway Cartage Agents, and Hamilton Bridge Company. He also had a notable military career, serving as a colonel in the Second World War in spite of the fact that he was past the age limit for service. He, too, inherited his father's love of race horses, and was for many years a director of the Ontario Jockey Club, and later its president.

In 1931, to celebrate the 100th anniversary of William Hendrie's birth, the family gave the breeding farm to the Royal Botanical Gardens. At the same time, they commissioned the master ironworker, Frederick John Flatman, to design and build the wrought iron gates which stand in the rose garden at the Royal Botanical Gardens. The gates are appropriately designed with symbols that Hendrie would have appreciated – a sheaf of durham wheat, a cluster of Ontario grapes, and a horseshoe.

On the grounds at the Royal Botanical Gardens, you can see the Fifteen-Mile marker for *The Herald* Around-The-Bay-Race which began in 1894. The race was established by J.M. Harris, publisher of *The Herald* and his brother, R.B. The two made a practice of walking the 19 miles around the Bay on Sunday mornings, and they often stopped at the Hendrie stables for a visit. When mile markers were being laid down, it was logical that one of them should be on the property of their friend, William Hendrie. The Five-Mile marker can be seen by the driveway at Dynes Hotel on Beach Boulevard.

Many famous runners took part in the race over the years – Tom Longboat, Charlie Bates, Jack Caffrey and Billy Sherring among them. J.M. Harris himself refereed the race and fired the starting pistol every year until his death in 1922. The race is still held annually, with two notable changes. There are now sometimes over 1,000 participants, and the name has been changed several times.

CARROLL, Peter

A neighbour of the Hendries at Valley Farm was Peter Carroll, after whom Carroll's Point in Hamilton Bay was named. Carroll was born near Ingersoll, Ontario in 1806. He studied surveying, then came to Hamilton to work as a road builder and contractor for the city's founder, George Hamilton. In the 1840s, he lived in a cottage called Bay View on the north shore of the Bay. Then he purchased 40 acres in the extreme southwest corner of East Flamborough. The point of land which juts out into the Bay from this property came to be known as Carroll's Point.

The property itself and the large house which Carroll built there from Queenston stone was called Rock Bay, after Peter Rock who was an early settler and tavern keeper in the area. The entrance to Rock Bay was a long, tree-lined driveway flanked by two gate houses on Plains Road.

Peter Carroll became a director of the Great Western Railway, the Gore Bank, and the Bank of Hamilton. In 1860, he was president and principal stockholder of the Brantford Bank, and president of Hamilton Oil Company. On two occasions, he ran in federal elections as the Tory candidate, but both times he was defeated. However, Carroll was highly respected as a man of integrity. In his will, Mahlon Burwell with whom he had studied surveying wrote, "In the event of any dispute....dispute is to be referred to Peter Carroll whose ruling will be final and binding on the disputants."

Peter Carroll and his wife, Henrietta, had many friends, and gave many lovely parties at Rock Bay. There is a story that when the suspension bridge was being constructed at Niagara Falls, Carroll, as a stockholder, arranged for his wife and some friends to cross the gorge in a basket. They got stuck half way across, to the alarm of all. Henrietta, always a perfect lady, begged her companions' forgiveness, let out one scream, then settled back to await rescue.

The Carrolls had no children. In 1876, Peter went to England, and on his return it was discovered that he had smallpox. He died at Rock Bay soon after. Henrietta lived there until her death. The house stood empty until 1908 when it was destroyed by fire. The remaining stone was used to build archways in the area, or was broken up as road material. The Rock Bay property forms part of what is now Woodland Cemetery.

READHEAD, John

At the turn of the century, the village of Lowville was a very busy place indeed. John Readhead ran a sawmill there. During the summer months, he would travel around the area buying large trees for timber. During the winter months, the mill was hard at work cutting lumber. The first saw mill was built in Lowville in the early 1800s. It burned in 1890, and was replaced by a new mill.

The village also had two blacksmith shops and a harness shop. However, in 1916, Mr. Readhead bought his first car — a model T with electric starter. It cost $600. With the coming of the automobile, harness-making and blacksmithing became almost obsolete.

Lowville Section Number Nine Public School at that time was a one-room school. In recent years, Maurice Readhead recalled that all the children walked to classes. The building was heated with a wood box stove in the centre of the room, and the children vied for a seat close to it in winter! Punishment for misbehaviour was staying in after school, or for serious transgressors, the strap.

The Readheads were active in community life. Charles Readhead who had a 100 acre farm on Walker's Line was warden of Halton County for many years, as well as serving on the Nelson Township council for 16 years, including two terms as deputy reeve, and six years as reeve. Back in 1917 when he began his political career, councillors were paid $3 a day and mileage one way when attending a township council meeting. Meetings often lasted all day. Charles Readhead also served on the Nelson Township School Board for 14 years. Born on a farm in Agnew's Hollow at the top of Walker's Line, Mr. Readhead was the son of a lumberman who had also been a member of the township council.

AUCKLAND, Fred

Clara and Fred Auckland took over the Lowville general store in 1937. In those days, they had a big pot bellied stove. So many of the local men were out of work because of the Depression that the store and the stove became the social centre of the community. Every day the menfolk would gather to chat and smoke.

Meanwhile, the Aucklands were busy carrying on local commerce. They stocked almost everything. Each week, they travelled three routes, making deliveries and buying produce from farmers. Often, farmers would barter chickens, butter or eggs for other goods that they needed. Eggs sold in the store for 15 cents a dozen. The original general store at Lowville was built between 1853 and 1858 by Andrew Pickett. The store later burned down, and was replaced by the present building. At one time, the store also served as post office, and had a cheese-making facility in the basement. The village's first telegraph service was operated from the building beginning in 1868.

Before taking over the general store, Fred Auckland was an employee of the Nelson Township Telephone Company which had its office on the Guelph Line at Highville, on the hill above Lowville. The office also employed two female switchboard operators. The telephone came to Lowville in 1909. The annual subscription fee for users was $15.00. By April, 1910, there were 95 phones in Nelson, Trafalgar, East Flamborough and Nassagaweya, and the demand continued to grow.

After the demise of the Nelson Township Telephone Company, Lowville residents were divided between the Burlington and Milton exchanges, with toll charges between them. This was a great inconvenience for everyone. A phone from each exchange was installed in the United Church parsonage for the convenience of the minister. However, the minister's wife soon found herself called upon to pass along messages from one exchange to the other to save the callers the toll charge. The problem was solved eventually by toll-free service between Burlington and Milton.

The Aucklands retired from the general store in 1961, but the historic little store is still a thriving business. It is now owned by Chris Madentzidis and his daughter who provide tea room and take-out service as well as an outdoor grill in warm weather.

WILLIAMSON, Edward

Edward Williamson, Burlington's funeral director, was a member of an early pioneer family in the community. He was probably first a carpenter, for he built coffins in the shop behind his funeral home on Brant Street. His son, Edgar, opened his own funeral establishment in 1903 at 372-74 Brant Street, next to the present Coronation Hotel. As many small-town funeral directors did, Mr. Williamson combined his business with a furniture store. The family lived in the apartment over the furniture store. Two daughters, Beulah and Violet, were born there. When Halley's Comet was visible in 1910, Beulah was taken out on the back porch to see it. The funeral business later moved north on Brant Street, and was eventually sold to W. Smith. The Smith Funeral Home now operates near the corner of Brant and Caroline Streets.

When his wife died in 1912, Edgar and the two girls moved farther up Brant Street to live with his parents. They were very strict Methodists who attended Sons of Temperance meetings at the present Sea Cadet Hall. This phase of their lives influenced the girls greatly.

Eventually, Edgar Williamson bought a house on Locust Street, next to the present Wingfield office building. He paid $3,500 for the house. At that time, taxes were $35.07 per year, and water cost $2.85. The house was sold during the Depression for $4,000.

The Williamson girls had many good times while growing up in Burlington. In winter, they enjoyed sleigh-riding, and skating out-of-doors on ice skates which fitted over their boots and were tightened with a key. Often, they skated on Brant's Pond, but in 1910 an outdoor rink was installed behind the Methodist Church on Elizabeth Street. When a hockey game was scheduled, Lloyd Moore would ring a bell and announce the event. In summer, the girls were allowed to go

Grandpa Williamson in 1936, at age 90 years.
—*Courtesy Beulah Tuck*

Beulah and Emily Williamson.
—*Courtesy Beulah Tu*

A horse-drawn hearse of Mr. Williamson.   —*Courtesy Jewel Johns*

down to the lake — but no farther than "the second tower" — to splash in the water. Often, with a group of friends, they would play croquet on the vacant lot next to their grandparents' home. On Sundays, however, all of these activities were forbidden.

Edgar's purchase of a Ford car in 1913 was met with disapproval by his mother. However, as time went by, she learned to appreciate this extravagance.

Brant Street was a two-lane street, but only half was paved as far as Highway 5. There was a board sidewalk on the east side of the street, but none at all on the west side until paving was done in 1923. A favourite excursion for the children was to walk from Brant Street through Bell's bush and Pettit's bush to the Guelph Line. This was especially popular in springtime when the wildflowers were in bloom.

Another branch of the Williamson family was well-known in the farming community on Walker's Line. John and Hannah Williamson farmed across the road from Hannah's father, Hiram Walker. Their daughter, Emily, became a lawyer and for many years lived and practised from the house on Lakeshore Road which became the Alice Peck Gallery.

In March, 1911, a double tragedy hit this family. First, Helen, widow of David Williamson, suffered a fatal stroke at her home on Lakeshore Road. Then, while preparing to attend his mother's funeral, W.J.S. Williamson, age 36, died suddenly from a severe attack of appendicitis. He was a popular member of the Victoria Football Club and the Nelson Beach golf club.

WAUMSLEY, Tom

For many years, the name Waumsley was well-known in the Brant Street business community. The family came from Oakville in 1929, and took over the bakery at Brant and Pine Streets, living in an apartment upstairs. In those days, the customer was always right, and the business thrived.

As a teenager, Flossie Waumsley worked at the Carroll's grocery store on Brant Street where the Toronto Dominion Bank is now located. After school, boys on bicycles delivered orders to the surrounding area, including Roseland. When the A & P store became self-serve in 1938, Flossie was the first

CAROLINE STREET W.		CAROLINE STREET E.

```
CAROLINE STREET W.                          CAROLINE STREET E.

Warry Residence                   Lynnhurst Motors
Dr. W.A. Bodkin, M.D.             Studebaker Dealer
A.L. Bailey, P.T.                 Edgecombe Ladies' Wear
St. Luke's Rectory                Edgewater Sports Centre
(Reverend Tebbs)                  Smith's Funeral Home
Dr. Walker, D.D.S.                MacDougall's Fuel & Supply Ltd.
Brant Bowling Alleys              Frank Armstrong's Menswear
Smith & Greenberg                 J. Bakers' Barber Shop & Pool Hall
Chrysler Dealer
Tuck Electrical Appliances        MARIA STREET

                                  H. Cleaver's Law Office
ONTARIO STREET                    (Masonic Temple)
                                  A & P Food Market
                                  TD Bank
Dr. W. Weaver                     Campbell's Drug Store
Town Hall                         Hyslop & Cole Dist. Smallwares
Burlington Library                Sani-Dairy
Federal Post Office               L. Utter Real Estate & Insurance
King Chinese Laundry              Burlington Bakery
Jack Duke Barber Shop             Boddington's Gift Shop
Sherwood Inn                      Mallet's Book Store
                                  Waddell's Insurance
                                  Wall's Meat Market
ELGIN STREET                      Olsen's Appliances
                                  Taylor Bros. Grocery Store
                                  Robin's Dry Goods
Hydro
Park                              JAMES STREET
Coronation Hotel
Wilbur Smith Furniture            Izard's Drug Store
Burlington Gazette                Smith's Hardware Store
Perkins Barber Shop & Pool Hall   Haswell's Furntiure Store
Burlington Dry Cleaners           Bush's Men's Wear
Robinson's Barber Shop            Coffee Pot Restaurant
Crown Cabs                        Harry Saunders'Shoe Store
Leo Waumsley's Restaurant         Watson' Jewellery
Callahan's Shoe Store             Hydro Office & Yard
                                  "Red" J. Waumsley's Supertest Station
                                  Anderson's Rest. & Fruit Store
Virtue Motors      Shell          Deluxe Taxi
Chevrolet Dealer   Station        Stedman's 5¢ & 10¢ Store
                                  Fasullo's Burlington Fruit Market
                                  Shower's Meat Market
                                  Lilly's Hat Shoppe
                                  Modern Shoe Repair
                                  Waumsley's Home Bakery
                                  Dale's Hardware Store

                                  PINE STREET

                                  Shaver's Drug Store
                                  Mel Howden's Shoe Store
                                  Tom Waumsley's Book Store
                                  Hucker's Dry Goods
                                  Carroll's Grocery Store
                                  Le Patourel's Drug Store
                                  (Dr. N. Mitchell, M.D.)
                                  Royal Bank
```

BRANT STREET

WATER STREET (NOW LAKESHORE ROAD)

Parker's Cleaners	Animal Hospital	Niagara Brand Spray Co.	Canadian Canners Factory

check-out girl — a new word in the Burlington vocabulary. When Flossie's husband, Jock Harrow, returned from war service in 1945, the young couple took over the bakery from her parents and operated it until 1969. It was a custom for them to give the wedding cake for every family wedding. When Jock's niece, Grace Almas, married the son of Albert England and Frances Waumsley, they remarked that since they were related to both the bride and the groom, for this occasion they had to give only one cake instead of two!

Other members of the Waumsley family were prominent on Brant Street, too. Flossie's brother Tom operated a magazine and smoke shop half a block from Water Street (Lakeshore) on the east side of Brant Street. This store had a small back room that was a delight for children because it was packed with the latest Big Little Books, cut-out doll books, and toys of every description. The store was also famous among local children for selling the best butterscotch ever made! Tom Waumsley managed the shop at first. Then the owner, Tom Jocelyn, went to England for a holiday, leaving Waumsley in charge. Mr. Jocelyn became ill on his return, and subsequently Tom Waumsley purchased the business.

Fred Parkin, who had the barber shop and pool room across from Waumsley's, had a well-known dog who crossed the road daily to pick up the newspaper for his owner. The dog would carry over carefully wrapped coins, and return with the newspaper, occasionally putting it down for a moment en route while he paused for an encounter with another dog.

For many years, Tom Waumsley was a member of the Burlington Volunteer Fire Brigade. He said that since his family lived across from the fire hall, the fire bell often woke him up, and he decided he might as well join the brigade. His father and his two brothers were also members of the fire brigade.

Jim Waumsley had Red's Garage; Albert owned a restaurant, and brother-in-law, Albert England, was proprietor of a meat market – all on Brant Street. The garage was across from the present Sims Square; the restaurant is now Lum's.

Waumsley Bakery, Brant St.

Lower Brant St. showing Graham's Shoe Store.

GRAHAM, Henry

For almost three-quarters of a century, Graham's Shoe Store was remembered as the place where baby got his first pair of white boots, or the teen-ager went with Mom to buy her first high heels. The store on Brant Street was originally Bell Brothers leather and harness shop. In 1906, it was bought by Henry Graham who moved the shop across the street in 1909. Graham had come from Hamilton where he had worked at a wholesale warehouse, then as a traveller.

In 1932, his nephew, Mel Howden, came from Alberta to work at the store. When Henry Graham died after World War Two, Mel Howden continued to operate the store until it was finally closed in 1979.

TAYLOR BROTHERS

Back in 1903, the elite in Burlington could pick up the telephone, ask for 41, and order nearly all of their household needs from Taylor Brothers. The store was built in 1902 by Fred and Charles Taylor on the site of the present I.G.A. Store at Lakeshore and Elizabeth Street.

The store was 100 feet long, 60 feet wide, and contained everything the average householder needed. There were groceries, dry goods, men's furnishings, coal oil for cooking and much, much more. Deliveries were made by horse and wagon, although in 1912 a motorized truck was used. On Saturday nights, the store closed at 11, then deliveries continued until 2 or 3 a.m.

In those early days, some of the Taylor Brothers staff who were known to everyone in town were Eddie Somers, Jack Troughten, Kate McGrath, Etta Filman and Stewart Taylor. W.W. Currie, another employee, opened his own store in 1915, specializing in meats and oysters in season.

The Taylor's store burned in 1912 when Tom Green lit a match near an oil drum. Of course, it was rebuilt, and in 1927 the business moved to Brant and James Streets where the lumberyard had been.

Charles Taylor died a year after the store was opened. F.W. lived until 1937, and his wife kept the business until 1949. At that time, the business sold for $65,000.

The Taylor Bros. delivery wagon.   —*Courtesy Joseph Brant Museu*

Ice cutting on the bay in 1926.   —*Courtesy Joseph Brant Museu*

Bruce Gibson started with Taylor Brothers at the age of 11 as a delivery boy. In 1950, he purchased a grocery business from his cousin, on the southeast corner of New Street at Guelph Line. Gibson's was well-known for 21 years, until the property was expropriated by the town.

MILNE, Frank

For 40 years, the Milne family carried on the coal business that was started around 1867 by George Allen. Fuel was only a part of Allen's enterprise. He owned a large hardware store at the corner of Brant and Pine Streets. The coalyard was behind the store at Pine and John Streets. Later, the coal business passed into the hands of Phil Patriarche, then F.W. Watson, before being bought by the Milnes in 1928.

When Frank Milne took over, there were only five employees, plus Mrs. Milne and his brother. They had four trucks which brought coal from a yard near Clarkson for $10 a ton. The coal originated in Pennsylvania, West Virginia and Kentucky, and was delivered to homes within a ten mile radius of Burlington. Coal was also purchased by greenhouse operators, and local industries such as Canadian Canners.

As the coal business was seasonal, in summer, the Milnes provided another seasonal service, ice delivery. Frank Milne remembers that ice was cut on the Bay in winter, and stored in four ice houses. One of these was on the beach near the present Joseph Brant Museum, two were on Maple Avenue at the end of Elgin, and one was on John Street near James. The ice was sold in the summer to supply ice boxes in Burlington homes.

Mr. Milne's wife, Mae Holtby, also came from a distinguished family. She came from England with her parents in 1912. They settled first in Winona, moving to Burlington in 1918. Edmond Holtby was a farmer who became interested in local politics, and served as mayor of Burlington in 1929-30.

GRAHAM, Chris

When Chris Graham was only two years old, he came to Burlington to live with his grandparents on their farm at the Guelph Line and Highway 5. He attended S.S. #5, on the

Chris Graham at door of his Brant St. Store, around 1950.—*Courtesy Paul Graham*

Birge-McNichol property open house after City of Burlington purchased it.
—*Courtesy Burlington Spectato*

northeast corner of the intersection. There were only about 25 children in the school, often with only three to a grade. When his widowed father remarried in 1914, Chris went back to live with him at Norval.

However, by 1928, Chris was travelling as a salesman in wholesale hardware. He noticed that Burlington had the nicest homes and lacked slum areas, so he returned to Burlington to live on Caroline Street. In 1949, he purchased Joe Smith's hardware store. In 1960, he sold this store to Osbaldestons and moved the business to 383 Brant Street. At about that time, his son Paul came into the business, taking it over when his father retired in 1971. At one time, there were five hardware stores on Brant Street. One of these was the original James Allen hardware and stove outlet, purchased from him in 1913 by Colton and Lorrimer.

Nowadays, many hardware stores and other specialty shops have disappeared. Department stores and malls sell everything, and offer plenty of parking space. As a result, smaller shops have often been put out of business. Shoppers who remember the era of small shops still miss the personal service and friendly associations that these businesses provided.

BIRGE, Cyrus

Cyrus Birge is connected with Burlington only through his descendants, but his is an interesting story. He was born in 1847 on a farm at Oakville. At 18, he went to work there in a dry goods store, while saving to attend medical school in Toronto. Unfortunately, ill health prevented him from completing his studies. He opened a grocery store in Stratford, then two years later went to work in the engineering department of the Great Western Railway. In 1882, he took over as manager of the Canada Screw Company in Dundas. The business was losing money, but as Birge rose through the ranks, he succeeded in turning it into a successful organization. In 1898, he purchased the company from its American parent firm and became its president.

It was soon after this that the mayor of Dundas imposed a $50 sewer charge on Canada Screw. Birge declared that he would not pay. The mayor gave him an ultimatum — "pay it or leave town". Birge took the challenge. One winter night, he had all of the company's machinery, tools and equipment loaded onto sleighs and removed from the Dundas location to a new site on Wellington Street North just below Barton Street in Hamilton. A few years later, Cyrus Birge's company merged with four others to create the Steel Company of Canada (STELCO). Birge was vice-president and a director of the new company.

When he died in 1929, Birge left a large fortune to his only surviving child, his daughter Edythe. With part of her inheritance, Edythe built Shoreacres, a stately mansion on Lakeshore Road between Appleby and Walker Lines. In addition to the house, the property had a playhouse, a gatehouse, a swimming pool, dock, tennis courts and lawn bowling greens. For many years, Edythe and her husband, J.J. MacKay enjoyed life in this lovely setting. When she died in 1960, Shoreacres went to her daughter Dorothy McNichol who lived in Hamilton and who used the family estate as a summer residence. Dorothy died in 1987, leaving the property to her five children. In 1990, Shoreacres was the subject of a court battle to determine whether or not it should be sold. In the end, it was purchased by the City of Burlington. The present proposal is to restore the house to its original grandeur, with the rest of the estate to be used as a park.

MCKINDLEY, Leonard

Among the early electricians in town was Leonard McKindley. He apprenticed in Toronto for five years, beginning when he was 15 years of age. For the first three years, he received no pay at all, while for the last year, he was paid three dollars a month.

Toward the end of the First World War, Leonard was drafted into the army, and served in Burlington as an electrician, then at the Brant Military Hospital as chief engineer. When he returned to civilian life, he began to specialize in automobile electrical systems which were "the coming thing" at that time. Since there was only one garage in town at the time, he was quickly hired to work there. The garage, at the corner of Locust and Water (Lakeshore) Streets, was operated by Charles Klainka who also had a large car repair shop on Pine Street.

Leonard McKindley was a man just a little ahead of his time, for he enjoyed inventing electrical gadgets, including an automatic timer for his stove. He was well-known in the area, and became president of the Garage Operators' Association of Ontario in 1945.

BRECKON, Earl V.

After John Breckon came to Canada from Yorkshire in 1831, other members of the family followed. His widowed mother came, along with her other children, Ester and Ralph Jr,. and his wife Lydia. There is a record of a Joseph Breckon and his wife Mary who were killed on a steamer when the boiler burst while going through the Lachine Rapids. Joseph was probably a brother of John, Ralph Jr. and Ester.

Joseph Breckon, the "Strawberry King", was a well-known Burlington farmer and reeve who lived until 1958, when he was 93 years old. He was descended from John and Isabella Breckon. His son, Earl Vernon became the founder of a well-known company which is still in operation.

Around 1930, Earl Breckon bought his first truck and began trucking fruit. As his business expanded to include other trucking jobs, he built a garage for his trucks beside his home on Plains Road, just west of Campbell's Corners (King and Plains Roads area). As careers sometimes do, his took a right turn, and he found himself in the concrete business, with two companies — Red-D-Mix Concrete and Mix Concrete Supply. His first major job was pouring the roadbed for the new High Level Bridge in 1932. The business gradually expanded until there were Red-D-Mix Concrete plants in London and St. Thomas, and Mix Concrete Supply plants in Hamilton, Guelph, Chippawa, Milton and other area cities. Red-D-Mix supplied the concrete for the Fanshawe Dam in London. In 1955, Red-D-Mix was sold to Standard Paving, but the Red-D-Mix name continues to be used.

Earl Breckon was also a partner of Andrew Peller in the establishment of Peller's Brewery on Burlington Street in Hamilton.

EASTERBROOK, Thomas

The name Easterbrook is best-known today for Easterbrook Avenue in Aldershot, and for Easterbrook's, the famous 12-inch hot dog stand on Spring Garden Road across the street from the Royal Botanical Gardens building. This well-known eating spot has been operating since 1930. For many years, Easterbrooks operated Willow Cove Post Office, serving the Brighton Beach area, in the same building where hot dogs, hamburgs and Cokes were served up.

When Brighton Beach was developed by W.D. Flatt in 1912, the residents used a power pumping system to provide their water supply. Mr. Easterbrook pumped water two or three times a year into a large cistern. Residents got their drinking water from this supply, or, if they worked in Hamilton, brought city water home in jugs. Homes had small cisterns to supply water for washing. It was with a sense of relief that Brighton Beach residents learned in 1950 that they would be receiving water from Burlington.

But the Easterbrook family came to Burlington long before all that. Thomas Easterbrook arrived in Canada in 1831, but didn't settle in Aldershot until 1859 when he purchased a large farm on the northeast corner at Campbell's Corners. The house on this property was an original Chisholm house, one of the oldest in Burlington. (The house, called Inverness, was razed in 1987, but has been reconstructed in Belleville.) At this family home, Thomas Easterbrook raised a large family. His brother, William, had a farm north of Plains Road on King Road, and also operated the toll gate at Campbell's Corners. These two busy gentlemen operated two brickyards and two sawmills. Thomas Easterbrook was also a member of Nelson county council in 1889 and 1890.

Another brother, John, had a farm west of the Oaklands property, extending from Plains Road to the Bay. There are still many Easterbrooks in the Aldershot area.

PATRIARCHE, William

The Patriarche family originally came to Canada from the Channel Islands. William Patriarche was a lawyer, and his wife Catherine gave music lessons. Two of their daughters married into the family of the Rev. Thomas Greene.

Later, Phil Patriarche was a well-known Brant Street business man who operated the fuel business established by George Allen many years before. The 1912 business directory tells us about his enterprises. It reads "Phil C. Patriarche — wholesale and retail dealer in hard and soft coal, wood cut and split, sewer pipes, cement, pressed brick etc. First class teams for hire. Phone office 23, residence 215."

KLAINKA, Charles

A newspaper clipping from August, 1910 tells us that a freak accident occurred at Nicholson's Planing Mill. A foreman, Charles Klainka, was sawing a board when a piece of wood broke off, hit the saw, flew off and struck him on the hand and stomach. He was knocked senseless, but recovered quickly. In a few minutes, he had his hand bandaged and went home.

Perhaps this incident convinced Mr. Klainka that work in the planing mill was too dangerous. Shortly after, we find that he operated the Ford Garage on the corner of Locust and Water (Lakeshore) Streets.

The Klainka (always pronounced Klankey) family had been residents of Burlington for a long time. In the late 19th century, Klainka's tailor shop was an established business at Highville, on the hill above Lowville. In the 1930s and 40s, another Mr. Klainka had the garbage collection contract for the beach strip.

VIRTUE, Frank

For almost 60 years, Frank Virtue played an important part in the business life of Burlington. He operated Virtue Motors on the northeast corner of Lakeshore and Locust Streets. Many residents remember buying their first automobile from him.

Earl V. Breckon in the 1950's.
—Courtesy
Elizabeth Breckon O'Hara

Virtue Motors.

—Courtesy Jack Vir

Virtue Motors, 1930.

—Courtesy Don Gibs

Frank Virtue was born in Enniskillen, north of Oshawa. After graduating from high school, he served as an apprentice at the R.S. McLaughlin Carriage Shop. He worked in Windsor for a while, then moved to Toronto where he started the Virtue and Liberty garage at 531 Yonge Street. He was determined to build cars, and borrowed money to finance his first project, a car with one front wheel. It was a disaster. Frank then decided that his place in the industry was in the maintenance and repair of cars. To prepare himself for the business side of this enterprise, he took correspondence courses in bookkeeping and administration from the Chicago Trade School.

In 1919, he moved to Burlington with his wife,Ethel,and their two children, Grace and Jack. A second daughter, Ruth, was born after their arrival here. Until 1921, the Virtues lived in a white frame house at the corner of Lakeshore and Locust, then they moved to 29 Hurd Avenue.

The new Ford dealership opened in a converted stable, with a frame house at the front serving as stock room and office. There were three people on the payroll. However, business was so good that by the following year there were eight employees. In the fall of 1922, the old house was torn down and a new garage was built. The following year, the adjoining service station was purchased so that customers were offered complete services for their vehicles.

In 1927, Virtue Motors switched from being a Ford dealership to General Motors. As business prospered, Frank Virtue decided to open a second dealership on Wentworth Street in Hamilton. General Motors refused to permit this, so Virtue Motors became a Chrysler dealer, and remained so until the business was sold to an employee, Joe Beaudoin, in 1975. The business is now operating on Fairview Avenue, while the original site of Virtue Motors is the Harborview condominium and business complex.

In 1930, Harold Hare, a Virtue Motors employee, tried the Radio College of Canada examination for radio servicemen. He achieved 96%, the highest mark ever given in Ontario. Thereafter, the company was also able to offer an up-to-date radio service department for customers.

Frank's son, Jack, chose a career as an eye, nose and throat specialist, practising for many years in Hamilton. He has many warm memories of his father who was a health fanatic, long before it became fashionable. He exercised before an open window every morning. Breakfast consisted of a glass of homemade tomato juice and a bowl of Dr. Jackson's Roman Meal cereal. His motto was "Every day, in every way, I feel better and better." He enjoyed fishing, and with his wife, Ethel, played badminton and lawn bowls.

During the Depression, Frank Virtue extended credit to many of his customers, especially farmers who needed gasoline and oil for their trucks in order to get produce to market. It was his belief that he would receive full payment if he accepted small payments during the productive months. He was right, for good service was the key to his business success.

Frank Virtue prided himself on his ability to "fine tune" a motor. Jack recalls that when he was a boy, his father regularly participated in the Slow Car Race around the track at the Burlington fairgrounds, located at the west end of what is now Queensway Drive. The Virtue car always won because it was tuned to run very slowly without stalling.

In 1946, during the building of the Royal Bank at the corner of Lakeshore and Brant, the bank staff worked out of the office at Virtue Motors. The original bank vault was left intact during construction, and bank staff were escorted by armed policemen to make deposits in the vault.

ALDERSON, John

When Christopher and Margaret Alderson purchased part of the Ireland farm in 1905, Dundas Street was a mud road, and Nelson was a busy little settlement. The 85 acre farm was at the corner of Dundas Street (Highway 5) and the Guelph Line. On this farm, with its 13 room house facing Highway 5, the Aldersons raised a family of five daughters and one son.

When he was 18, John Alderson became an assistant to Ephraim Chapman, the local auctioneer. John's first opportunity to sell was at a quota sale. This meant that a person, holding a lien against a property, had foreclosed. When the quota, or amount of the loan, was reached, the auctioneer stopped selling. In this case, Ephraim Chapman was discouraged with the sales, and told John to try his luck with the cattle. John told the handlers to bring out the cattle in quick succession, and he sold the first cow to a low bidder to stimulate the crowd. It worked, and he was successfully launched on his career. In fact, when his father answered the telephone, he used to say "Chris Alderson here, father of the auctioneer."

John eventually bought out the Henderson auction business, and continued to practise his profession for 60 years. For many years, he was the only licensed auctioneer in Halton County, and he also held a licence in Wentworth County. During a one month period in the fall of 1920, John had to refuse sales because he was already booked for each working day of the month. In the Depression years, he had to preside at many mortgage sales. He disliked this aspect of his work, and often tried to help farmers make last-minute arrangements to avoid foreclosure.

Florence Meares remembers that John Alderson auctioned off 35 head of registered Holstein cattle on her father's farm in 1925. He was a very good humoured man, and lived up to his reputation for knowing how to work the good will of the crowd.

In 1919, John married the local schoolteacher, Zetta Bousfield, and they moved into part of his parents' house on the farm on the corner of Highway 5 and Guelph Line. John then purchased the Nelson store located on the northwest corner of the same intersection, and turned it into a thriving business. Electricity had not reached the community, but John installed lighting, powered by a generator. During the next few years, he also purchased other properties in Nelson.

When John's mother died, he and his family moved back to Alderson Estates farm where he carried on mixed farming. For many years, he shipped cream to the Creamery in Milton, and later maintained a herd of beef cattle.

The property adjoined that of St. John's Anglican Church, and for many years John was active in that parish. He gave land to the cemetery board to increase the size of the burial ground, and served as rector's warden for 32 years.

John M. Alderson selling a mon
box, around 1949.
—*Courtesy Howard Alders*

Nicholson & Son plant, around 1930.　　　　　　—*Courtesy George Hawl*

The Aldersons' two storey, white frame house was demolished in 1971 when Highway 5 was widened for the fourth time. Fortino's Plaza at the corner of Guelph Line and Coventry Way is now located on the site of the Alderson farm. Alderson Court and Alder Drive in this area are named for the Alderson family.

When John's son, Howard, was a boy, he helped his father by posting sales bills on dozens of telephone poles, and in local businesses. There was a lot of work in preparing for a sale which could last from 10 a.m. until evening. All the items to be sold had to be listed and evaluated, notices had to be printed at the Gazette office, and advertising had to be prepared. The auctioneer was usually paid a percentage of the receipts, ranging from two per cent to ten per cent, depending on the type of sale.

At the age of 18, Howard followed in his father's footsteps. He became an auctioneer, and the two became a popular team with a loyal following in the community.

The Aldersons were a musical family. John had what he called the Alderson Orchestra. He played the violin, his sister Margaret (Mrs. Arthur Peer) played piano, and his sister Louise (Mrs. Fred Harbottle) played cello. John's violin, bearing the inscription "1639, Coruna, Italy" was purchased for $9 in a Hamilton pawnshop!

John Alderson was born on Friday, March 13th, 1881, and died on Friday, October 13th, 1967.

NICHOLSON, Allan

Allan S. Nicholson was born in 1882 on his father's farm near Waterdown. As a young man, he followed in the footsteps of other young farmers of that era, going west each year to work on the fall harvest on the prairies. One year, instead of coming home for the winter, he went to British Columbia and worked at a lumber operation.

In 1907, he decided that he preferred the lumber business to farming. With his father's assistance, he purchased James Harrison's planing mill and lumber yard on Brant Street opposite the eastern end of Ontario Street. The down payment was $1,000.

Thus Nicholson Lumber Company was established. The original office was a hotel, the Burlington Inn, adjacent to the yard. Later, the business and the hotel were moved west on Ontario Street to a site between Maple Avenue and the Canadian National Railway right-of-way.

At the end of the First World War, Mr. Nicholson became associated with a Toronto wholesale lumber company named Terry and Gordon. The Nicholson family moved to Toronto in 1921. The company's name was changed to Terry, Nicholson and Cates, then in 1931 to Nicholson and Cates. In 1939, the Nicholsons moved to Burlington, and shortly after the company relocated here as well.

While the Nicholson family lived in Toronto, the Ontario Street operation was managed by O.W. Rhynas who had an interest in the company. The company was called O.W. Rhynas and Son, Limited. When Mr. Rhynas died in the 1930s, the name became A.S. Nicholson and Son, Limited.

During the Second World War, Mr. Nicholson was called to Ottawa to work with the Timber Control Board which was established to mobilize the nation's timber resources. Mr. Nicholson served first as deputy timber controller, then as timber controller, before returning to Burlington and his own business interests.

In 1945, he ran as federal Progressive Conservative candidate in the Halton riding, but was defeated in the election by his good friend, Hughes Cleaver. For many years, he was a member of the Public School Board. During his term as chairman, the new high school was built on Brant Street, and the new Lakeshore School was constructed.

No doubt being very aware of the damage fire can do, especially in a lumber yard, Allan Nicholson became a member of the volunteer fire brigade. In 1911, he was chief, and later served as secretary-treasurer.

He is perhaps best remembered, however, as chairman of the first board of governors of Joseph Brant Memorial Hospital. The need for a hospital in Burlington had been under discussion for many years. The time had passed when women expected to have their babies born at home, and accident victims were no longer treated on the scene or in a doctor's

nside Nicholson plant. —Courtesy *Joseph Brant Museum*

Allan S. Nicholson & staff, 1909. —Courtesy *Joseph Brant Museum*

office. Yet it was not practical to expect people to travel to Hamilton or Toronto for hospital care.

In 1955, a steering committee was established, with M.M. Robinson as chairman. The committee lobbied for support which was overwhelming in the community, and plans for the hospital began to take shape. There was some controversy over the choice of a site for the hospital. One group of citizens wanted it to be built on the northwest corner of Upper Middle Road and Guelph Line where the present Halton Board of Education Offices are now located. At that time, the area was underdeveloped, and it was difficult to visualize a hospital on the outskirts of town. There was a great deal of heated discussion at a public meeting, and finally the decision was made in favour of the present location on the site of the former Brant Military Hospital.

In January, 1958, the first board of governors was elected, with Allan S. Nicholson as chairman. The hospital was named in memory of that property's first owner, Joseph Brant. The six storey building was constructed at a cost of $3,700,000, and opened its doors in February, 1961. An addition was added in 1966, but again in the 1990s, the Joseph Brant Memorial Hospital is in need of further expansion.

Allan Nicholson was also the first president of the Halton and Peel Trust and Savings Company which was later purchased by Canada Trust Company.

The Nicholsons had one son, Warren, who was born in 1915 in the house on the northwest corner of Brant and Ontario Streets. After completing his education at the University of Toronto, Warren, like his father before him, went to British Columbia. For three years, he worked for various logging and lumber operations. When he returned home in 1937, he joined Nicholson and Cates as a lumber salesman. Two years later, he became general manager of the millwork factory in Burlington.

From the end of the war until the death of Allan Nicholson, father and son worked closely in the family business. In 1947, a profit sharing pension plan was introduced for employees, based on that established by DOFASCO. In the mid-1950s, a new factory was built on the North Service Road for the manufacture of structural timber, arches and glued laminated timber products.

After Allan Nicholson's death in 1964, some of the company's assets were sold. In 1967, a group of employees took over the manufacturing division of A.S. Nicholson & Son Limited which at that time had a staff of about 400 people. The company operated under the name of Nicholson Building Components Ltd., and was Canada's largest manufacturer of windows, stairs and pre-hung exterior doors. Products were shipped all over North America and abroad. The company operated on the lumber yard's original six acre site on Ontario Street with the old Burlington Inn as the main office building. However, the company went into receivership in 1970, and assets were auctioned off. The old hotel building was demolished in 1971.

The retail lumber and building supply yard on the southeast corner of New Street and Guelph Line was not sold. It remained under the management of Warren's brother-in-law, James Morton. In 1973, this business was expanded, and relocated on the northeast corner of Walker's Line and Fairview Street. Nicholson and Cates (Burlington) Limited is still a wholesale lumber company operated on Heritage Road by the Nicholson family.

PEGG, Leonard

For nearly 70 years, the Pegg family owned the Dakota Mill, just south of the village of Kilbride on Cedar Springs Road. The mill was built sometime in the 1840s, and was used both for grinding grain and for sawing lumber. At that time, the hamlets of Dakota and nearby Cumminsville were thriving settlements.

There is a legend about the mill's name. Apparently, a group of Dakota Indians was camped nearby with some government surveyors. When it was time for them to move on, a young Indian girl was too ill to go with them. A local family took care of her, and eventually she married one of the sons. They lived in a small house across the creek from the mill site. When the mill was built, it was named "The Dakotah Mill" in honour of the Indian maiden.

The Pegg family purchased the mill and about five acres of property in 1911. The last owner of the mill was Leonard Pegg who continued to use the water-powered mill to cut custom-ordered lumber. When Mr. Pegg considered selling the mill in 1978, he had a clause incorporated into the deed stating that the building could not be torn down. In August, 1979, the mill was sold to a man who planned to turn it into a restaurant. An auction was held, and Mr. Pegg's collection of old automobiles and other memorabilia was sold. Unfortunately, Mr. Pegg did not live to see his mill restored and renovated. Nor did the mill survive. On November 17th, 1979, it burned to the ground. Its site is marked by a plaque.

SINCLAIR, William

William Sinclair and his wife, Jean Gordon, were natives of Kirkcudbright, Scotland. They married in 1801, and emigrated to the United States, coming to Canada after the War of 1812. On reaching Nelson Township, they purchased 140 acres of land from John Brant. This property was on the east side of Brant Street, three miles north of Wellington Square. It was heavily wooded, and wolves and other wild animals abounded. In 1830, William built a one storey stone house which he called Grey Stone Villa.

William and John Brant became close friends. For many years, the owners of the house retained the table at which Brant dined shortly before one of his trips to England. Before his trip, Brant invited William to go home with him to see the outfit he would wear when he met the monarch. On this trip, Brant made a point of writing to the Scottish poet, Thomas Campbell who, in his poem, *Gertrude of Wyoming*, had referred to John's father as "the Monster Brant" because of supposed atrocities committed at the battle of Wyoming. Brant was able to prove to Campbell that this claim was unjust. Campbell apologized, and later his apology was published in *The New Monthly Magazine* for all to read.

William's son, David, inherited the Grey Stone Villa farm on Brant Street. Another son, Robert, was one of the first businessmen in Aldershot. In 1856, he opened a shoemaker's business on the southwest corner of LaSalle Park Road and

Plains Road. In 1898, Robert's son, George, became postmaster at Aldershot, thus beginning a family tradition. His son, Bruce, was postmaster until 1956 when he was transferred to the Burlington post office. Bruce's sister, Jean, then became post-mistress.

In addition to running the post office, George Sinclair operated a grocery business on the same premises. For many years, he supplied area residents with many of their basic needs. In 1911, he advertised new currants, new raisins and new peels. Sweet cider was available at his store for 10 cents a quart, and Wagstaffe's mincemeat was also advertised. Sinclair was well liked, for he often carried the farmers through the spring, accepting payment only when their first crop of strawberries had gone to market.

William and Jean's eldest son, Samuel, became a carpenter. He married Margaret Clarkson of Hamilton. In 1845, it is recorded that Lewis Horning sold Samuel 125 acres of land in Nelson Township on the second concession north of Dundas Street. This farm was later owned by Samuel's son, John Clarkson Sinclair who had two sons and a daughter.

The first of these sons, Samuel, took a business course at Canada Business College in Hamilton, then went to Nebraska to become a master butter-maker. He then returned to the family farm and married Catherine Shields of Lowville. In 1903, the farmers of Nelson village formed an association to build a creamery and produce butter. The creamery was constructed on the south side of Dundas Street, just east of St. John's Anglican Church. Samuel Sinclair was engaged to operate it. Sinclair bought the house and property on the northeast corner of Dundas Street and the Guelph Line, and moved his family there to be closer to the creamery.

Samuel was an ingenious person. He was one of the first in the community to have a hot air furnace installed in his home for central heating. He also installed acetylene lighting throughout the house. He owned one of the first automobiles in the area, a McLaughlin Buick. Since farm horses were unaccustomed to automobiles, occasionally a farmer would ask Samuel to drive around the village for a short while so that a spirited carriage horse could become used to this modern distraction.

The Sinclair home had one of the first telephones in the area. Often, a physician or veterinarian visiting the area would arrange a signal system between their offices and Catherine Sinclair. When a message came, Catherine would place a white sheet outside an upstairs window which was plainly visible from the crossroads. This would tell the doctor that a message was waiting for him at the Sinclair home.

When the visiting dentist came to town, he would usually get in touch with a farmer in a central location, and arrange for neighbours to be notified and appointments made. Since anaesthetics were not available, the dentist gave each patient a good-sized glass of whiskey prior to extractions.

Around 1911, when marketing butter became more competitive, Samuel Sinclair was offered a job as master butter-maker at L.O. Buist, a large Hamilton firm. He moved his family into Burlington and commuted to work on the Hamilton-Burlington Electric Railway. The local farmers' association closed down the Nelson creamery. In 1914, Samuel changed his vocation, entering the retail lumber business, first with A. Coates and Sons, and later with Allen S. Nicholson. Both of Samuel's and Catherine's sons, Gordon and Jonathan, became medical doctors and had outstanding careers in this field.

SPRINGER, Byron

In the early 1900s, the village of Nelson was a busy community. The centre of activity was the general store and post office on the northwest corner of Guelph Line and Highway 5. This building was owned and operated by Byron Springer, son of David Warren Springer. The Springer family had been an integral part of Nelson village since 1835.

Byron Springer's red brick store had a platform which went around two sides of the building. Iron rings were set into the platform so that farmers could tie their horses when visiting the store. The store was a popular meeting place where the men would gather on a Saturday evening to discuss the crops or the news. It was here that news of the sinking of the

Titanic first came to the village in 1912. The store was destroyed by fire in 1949.

On the southeast corner of the intersection was the farm owned by Edward Emerson. His large brick house had been Chisholm's Inn, and many dances had been held in the third floor ballroom. Next door to this house was the township hall where regular council meetings and other gatherings were held.

Across the road on the north side of Dundas Street was William Greer's blacksmith shop. Just east of it was a factory owned by James Bell. Farmers brought logs here to be made into wooden pumps. In 1916, the business was sold to Elgin Moore who operated it as a sawmill. He owned a large steam engine which was used to haul the first stone used in the construction of Dundas Street. Next to the factory was Frank Tuck's gas station where the men and boys congregated on Saturday nights to hear Foster Hewitt's hockey broadcasts.

On the southwest corner of the village was the creamery operated by Samuel Sinclair, and just beyond it, St. John's Anglican Church. Across the street was one of the oldest churches and burial grounds in the area — Nelson United Church. The first burial there was that of Mrs. Hugh McLaren who died while her husband was away fighting in the War of 1812. Another old church at Nelson is St. Paul's Presbyterian which celebrated its 170th anniversary in 1992.

HOWARD, John

John Howard grew up on his father's farm on Plains Road, west of Waterdown Road, with the Easterbrooks and the Unsworths as neighbours. Hiram Howard's farm had about 25 acres of cherry trees, and also produced a special strain of melons as well as tomatoes. John went to university to study classics, but in 1921, the start of a new business in the family required his help.

It seems that a teamster had heard that Hiram Howard's farm was sandy, and he asked for a load of this soil. John's help was required to dig a hole in the middle of the cherry orchard, and to shovel sand into the teamster's horse-drawn wagon. The man came back several times for more sand, and also told others where he was getting it. Since the farm was not very prosperous at that time, Hiram Howard gradually turned from farming to the sand and gravel business.

During the Second World War, a modern gravel and sand crushing and washing plant was built on the property. Around this time, Howard Concrete and Materials Ltd. produced an extra strong ready-mix concrete made by blending ground glass with the mix. Most of Howard's jobs were bridges and highways, as well as prefabricated concrete houses made from large slabs prepared on the site, then raised by cranes. Howard's own house was the first one made of concrete.

Howard concrete was also supplied for the Joseph Brant Memorial Hospital and the Canada Centre for Inland Waters. In 1972, the plant was sold to Canadian Building Materials, and the experimental division went to King Paving.

When John Howard moved from Hamilton to Aldershot to manage the family business, he built the boat house first, then the house! An avid boater, he was instrumental in starting a power boat instruction course in Burlington. His Aldershot home had a large garden, as well as grapes, peaches, pears and apricots. Using his special cement, his home had the first swimming pool in Burlington. The children loved to play on the sand piles at the plant which covered the area from Plains Road to the railway tracks, and from Waterdown Road to Howard Road. In the 1940s, a mastodon tusk was found on this property, and was donated to McMaster University's geology department.

COOKE, Jacob

Sometimes, lasting and successful businesses begin quite by accident. That seems to be the case with J. Cooke Concrete Block Limited which is still operating under the name TCG Materials Limited.

Jacob Cooke was born in England in 1908, and came to Canada in 1927. After trying Winnipeg, Orangeville, and Oakville, he finally settled down in Burlington. He worked as a carpenter's helper for Pigott Construction, specializing in the laying of hardwood floors. One of the jobs he worked on was at The Pig and Whistle on Lakeshore Road.

House with shed where first cement blocks were made, New St. at Martha.
—*Courtesy Bill Cooke*

Dakota Mill.   —*by Gery Puley*

Second Cooke plant.

—Courtesy Bill Coo[

Cooke truck — Frank Armstrong &
Cam Patterson, around 1949.
—Courtesy Frank Armstrong

Apple.
— —*Courtesy Muriel Hobson Rhinehart*

Pump house at bay, where water was obtained for the plant.   —*Courtesy Bill Cooke*

In 1935, Jake, as he was known, purchased a hand-operated block-making machine, and manufactured some concrete blocks in a shed at the back of his home at 3 New Street. The shed is still standing. The blocks were to be used as bases for Christmas trees that decorated Brant Street that Christmas season. Most of Jake's work was done at night, although on Saturday mornings he was often helped by Garnet Ireland. Police Chief Lee Smith fined him a number of times for disturbing the peace of a residential neighbourhood. In 1937, he installed his first power-operated block machine. He purchased sand and gravel from Frank Scheer on St. Matthews Avenue. The demand for concrete blocks continued, so what had begun as a small cottage industry expanded to larger premises on St. Matthews Avenue in Aldershot, on land purchased from George Filman. An adjacent 55 acre gravel pit provided the raw materials needed for the rapidly growing operation. At one time, a 15,000 year old mammoth tusk was uncovered by a power shovel excavating this quarry. The tusk was five feet long, and weighed 75 lbs. It was donated to the Joseph Brant Museum.

Brant Coleman worked for Jake Cooke from 1937 until his retirement. Since the two worked well together, they also bought property in Aldershot, Oakville and Hamilton, where they laid out streets, then sold to builders. In 1952, they developed the Glen Acres survey (Birdland) on the Filman property. Brant Coleman, Jake's secretary, Isabel, and Bill Cooke (Jake's son) named the streets after birds in honour of William Filman who had had a bird sanctuary on this property. In the Fairview Acres survey on North Shore Boulevard, Bill named the streets after his children — Daryl, David, Lynn, and Lee. He named William Court for himself, and Cullum Court for his stepmother's family. Barrymore Court is named after his brother, while Isabel Court and Coleman Court are in honour of the other name-choosers.

As the business expanded, Cooke bought Joe DeLuca's farm which is now the site of Cooke Industrial Park. He also bought the swamp area below the pool at Hidden Valley Park as a settling pond so that no contaminants from the gravel pit would enter the creek. Ken Sobel of CHML owned the property north of Hidden Valley Park and had the radio station's transmitter there. When Sobel decided to develop that area, Jake Cooke extracted the sand and gravel, then levelled the land ready for building.

By 1953, J. Cooke Concrete Block was the largest producer of concrete blocks in Canada, each day producing enough cement blocks to build 30 houses. The company was in operation around the clock, and produced ten million eight-inch blocks a year. Concrete block houses were built on Cooke's Lane and rented to employees. There was also a big bunk house with a restaurant open 24 hours a day. Jake Cooke was already building concrete block homes for sale. They sold for about $1,700 and were greatly in demand in the post-war era.

Cooke's pre-stressed concrete was used in the construction of the McMaster University athletic building and the Burlington City Hall. Every Tuesday when working on the city hall, Cooke's would put in a floor; then during the week the walls would go up ready for the installation of the next floor on the following Tuesday. Cooke's also supplied the panels on the outside of the city hall.

Jacob Cooke, retaining the land development company, sold the concrete block business in 1958 to two of his employees – Zedd Krajna who was the office manager and accountant, and Jack Easterbrook who was the lawyer for the company. Jake's son, Bill, stayed on to manage the company, with his brother Barry as plant manager. Two years later, the company installed autoclaves, high pressure curing vessels which stabilize the concrete blocks to prevent shrinkage. In 1977, the company was sold again, this time to TCG Materials Limited of Brantford. For many years, the company retained the name Cooke Concrete, although it has now been changed. The business continues to thrive on the site that Jacob Cooke chose on St. Matthews Avenue.

When he was 62, Jake Cooke went to Australia to visit cousins whom he had not seen since childhood. He discovered that it was still a pioneer country. Convincing his son, Barry, to sell his farm in Carlisle and join him, Cooke bought 28,000 acres of bush and scrub land in an area where the nearest telephone was 40 miles away. He cleared 14,000 acres, and by 1976 was able to plant 11,000 acres of grain. An Australian newspaper reported, "Canadian does in 5 years what takes an Australian 20 years."

Bill Cooke has continued to follow the family business. He developed 220 lots at Flamborough Hills of Carlisle, near his brother, Barry's, farm. The Cooke family developed over 800 residential lots in the Aldershot area, with Oaklands on the bayshore as the current project.

ANDERSON, Sam

In the early 1920s, Sam and Gertie Anderson, with their three daughters, moved from Bartonville to a five acre market garden on Maple Avenue. During the Depression of the 1930s, they lost the farm. Sam sold MacDonald's celery hearts from door to door. Sam and Gertie also had a fruit and vegetable booth on the beach strip across from the old brick pump house. Later, they moved the booth to the northwest side of Water Street at the Guelph Line.

In 1939, they opened a fruit and flower store at 387 Brant Street. This building had originally been a bakery, operated by C.H. Henley, and his father before him. At that time, the baking was done in brick ovens in the basement. A kitchen and living room were located at the rear of the main floor, with the rest of the living quarters upstairs. In 1933, John Dykstra opened the Burlington Bakery in the same building. When he moved his business to 433 Brant Street, the old building across from Hydro Park stood vacant until the Andersons took it over. They started out with six baskets of Lawrie Smith's apples, a crate of oranges, a case of "pop", and six potted plants.

The business prospered. Mrs. Anderson served as cashier, and in time daughters Muriel and Audrey took part in the business, too. When chain stores began to appear in the community and make inroads into the Anderson business, Muriel's husband, Curly Hobson, suggested that they might try serving coffee and Mrs. Anderson's delicious pies. A few stools were added, and gradually, Mrs. Anderson's cooking began to take precedence over the fruits, vegetables and groceries. Sam Anderson died in 1950, but his wife carried on, with the help of her daughters.

By 1955, Anderson's Brunch Bar was a restaurant exclusively, although the family continued to make up gift fruit baskets. Six-quart Glover baskets were decorated, filled, and cellophaned. At Christmas, they produced hundreds, priced from $2.50 to $5.00.

Anderson's restaurant was famous for its chile con carne. Produce was still provided by local farmers — George Beech's tomatoes, Hopkins' peaches, Stephensons' asparagus, Paul Lipinski's organic vegetables and blueberries, and "special" items from the gardens of Charlie Cole and Art Hayes. The Andersons also did catering, featuring fancy sandwiches and fruit and vegetable salads. The Brunch Bar was sold to a new owner in 1966.

Muriel and Curly Hobson made the news in 1974 when an apple tree in the garden of their Camborne Crescent home produced a Northern Spy 15 inches in circumference, and weighing two-and-three-quarters pounds. The tree, which was once part of an orchard, produced 30 baskets of apples, and drew the attention of fruit experts at the Vineland Research Station.

BYRENS, Emma

"A human document rich in contemporary history; a record of the most pleasant side of our times." This is the inscription on the first page of the guest book from the Estaminet Restaurant. It is certainly an accurate statement of the Estaminet's place in Burlington history.

Emma and George Byrens bought the old house at 2084 Lakeshore Road in 1919, and opened a restaurant with only four tables. Before long, they had established a reputation for serving fine food in an exceptionally pleasant lakefront atmosphere. Mrs. Byrens ordered all the supplies locally, and according to the farmers, she insisted on the best. Some of the ladies in town bought their preserves from her. An advertisement of the time for Burke's "Uneeda" ice cream boasts that this product is used exclusively at the Estaminet. It goes on

The Estaminet.

Students learning the restaurant business, around 1968.

to urge, "Take a large brick home with you at 35 cents. The Auto party brick at 10 cents is the latest ice cream sensation."

Mr. and Mrs. Byrens greeted their guests in full evening dress. Guests were also greeted by the lime green parrot, Paul, who resided in the lobby. Paul knew the staff members by name, and initiated conversations with anyone who came by. When the Metropolitan Opera performances were broadcast from New York, he loved to join in the chorus. At 11.30 p.m., and again at a quarter to twelve, he would call out "All out, gentlemen. This establishment is now closing!" Paul was believed to be seven or eight years old at the time. According to a clipping from *The Globe and Mail*, he was still living in Burlington in 1969.

The guest books from the Estaminet are filled with signatures of visitors from all over the world, some of them very famous. According to the books, visitors included Liberace, Louis Armstrong, John Diefenbaker, and Barbara Ann Scott. One year, on Mother's Day, Ontario Premier Mitchell F. Hepburn, with Mrs. Hepburn and a party of friends dined there. In May, 1931, Viscount Duncannon, son of Canada's new governor-general, Lord Bessborough, had dinner with a group of friends. After the meal, the viscount personally congratulated Mrs. Byrens on her excellent establishment.

Fellow restaurateurs honoured the Byrenses with visits, too. At Christmas, 1946, J. Murray Anderson and Mr. and Mrs. Cliff Kendall of the Brant Inn dined there. That same year, Peggy O'Neil from the Village Inn in Grimsby and W. Wright of the Granite Club in Toronto also paid visits to the Estaminet.

Many organizations chose this fine restaurant for their special dinners. Members of the Ontario Restaurant Association met there. Other groups included Ridley College, St. Paul's Church Choir of Toronto, the Wardens of Halton County, and the Reunion of the Class of 1885 from Central School in Hamilton.

A party was held for Emma Byrens in honour of the 20th anniversary of the Estaminet. In addition to bringing fame to Burlington, she contributed to the community in many other ways. In 1940, during World War II, she organized a card party for 400 guests with the proceeds going to the Burlington district branch of the Canadian Red Cross. Mayor Gordon Blair and Paul Fisher, president of the Burlington Red Cross, officiated at the draws. The program included dancing by the pupils of Miss Helen Kerr of Hamilton, after which Lee Smith, chief of police, auctioned off four cakes which went for "fancy prices." Hughes Cleaver, M.P., gave a brief history of Canada's war effort. The event raised $300.

In 1943, Mrs. Byrens celebrated her 70th birthday with another party at the Estaminet. She continued as proprietess of the restaurant until 1952. At that time, it was purchased by Reginald Cooper who, with his wife, operated it until 1963 when their son, Brian, took it over. It has since changed hands more than once.

HELLINGMAN, Theo

When Meta and Theodore Hellingman arrived in Burlington in 1951, they were unlike many of the other Dutch emigrants who came. They did not settle on a farm, nor did they join the Dutch Reformed or Canadian Reformed churches.

Theo, his parents and his brother and sister came from the Netherlands aboard the steamer *Southern Cross*. They were sponsored by friends in Burlington. At first, they rented a home at the corner of Lorne and Bridgman Avenues. Later, Mr. Hellingman Sr. bought a small farm at Appleby Line and New Street.

When the family arrived, there were three places in Burlington where these men could hope for employment — Nicholson's Lumber, Halliday's Lumber, and the Glover basket factory. Theo and his father worked first at Halliday's for 75 cents an hour. Theo later worked on the construction of the Ford plant in Oakville for $1 an hour, while his father was employed at the Aylmer Canning Factory on Lakeshore Road.

Meta also came from Holland, intending to stay only three months to visit her brother in Puslinch. Her visa was extended when she took a temporary position as nanny with a family in Hamilton. Through mutual friends, she met Theo, and they were married.

Theo Hellingman, parents, sister and brother, leaving their home in the Netherlands to come to Canada in 1951.
—Courtesy Meta Hellingman

Theo Hellingman on board ship coming to Canada to start a new life, 1951.
—Courtesy Meta Hellingman

Aerial view of the Cannery. Brant St. in background. —*Courtesy Joseph Brant Museu*

The Cannery. —*Courtesy Hamilton Public Libra*

Through the years since their marriage, they have been an industrious family, proud of being Canadian, while at the same time retaining their Dutch heritage.

LEITCH, Alexander

In March, 1902, Reeve William Kerns called council together to discuss the possibility of bringing to Burlington a company for milling or canning in order to enhance the village's industrial tax base. Consequently, the following year, the Burlington Canning Company was formed by a group of farmers and landowners. A factory was built on the waterfront between Brant and Elizabeth Streets, the site of the Venture Inn to-day. Two years later, council approved a radial line down John Street to service the canning company which had extensive offices and warehouses.

In 1910, the cannery was purchased by Dominion Canners Company. Alexander Leitch came to Burlington from Strathroy to manage the cannery. The Leitch family lived at the Queens Hotel while a house was built for them on Hurd Avenue. During this time, Mrs. Leitch caught scarlet fever and was taken to Toronto where she remained in quarantine for six weeks.

As manager of the cannery, it was Mr. Leitch's responsibility to get in touch with local farmers and arrange to buy their produce. Most of it came from the farms on Maple Avenue and along Plains Road. During the busy seasons, many Indians worked in the cannery. Mr. Leitch used to go to Caledonia to pick them up at the end of each week-end. Women came from as far away as Buffalo and Ohsweken to work at the cannery during the peak season. Most of them lived at the nearby "help house" which had 24 units.

In its early days, the cannery packed fruits, vegetables, meats, poultry, pork and beans, jams, jellies, catsups and relishes, with tomato pulp a specialty. Later, it was famous for its tomato catsup, applesauce and tomato juice, packed under the brand names Burlington and Vulcan. In the off-season, the staff packed olives imported from Spain, and spaghetti in cheese sauce. Finished products were exported to the

Canadian Canners from Lakeshore Blvd.

Bottling Ketchup at Canadian Canners, 1954.
—*Courtesy Joseph Brant Museum, Frank Wright Collection*

British Isles, Australia, Malta, Germany, France, British Honduras and the West Indies.

Everyone who lived in Burlington during the cannery's existence can remember the aroma of catsup during the canning season. Most people liked this smell, but one woman asked Mrs. Leitch to get her husband to "do something about the terrible smell."

About 1,000 tomato growers in the area sold their produce to the cannery for 25 cents a bushel. During the peak season, workers were on the job at 5 a.m., and worked 18-hour days. The tomatoes were put into 1,000 gallon stainless steel tanks which were heated by steam pipes. About 75 per cent of the ingredients boiled away before the product was completed.

In 1923, Aleck Leitch was moved to the head office of Canadian Canners in Hamilton. However, he still dropped in at the Burlington plant frequently. He had many friends among Burlington businessmen. Elgin Harris at the *Gazette* was a particularly good friend, and the two enjoyed sitting in the newspaper office and discussing the news of the day. Aleck Leitch was also a close friend of Tom Longboat, the famous Indian runner.

The cannery on the lakefront remained in operation until 1960. For many years, it was operated as a subsidiary of Canadian Canners under the name Aylmer Factory No. 36. During this period, it produced Aylmer tomato juice, catsup and tomato soup.

Tommy Thomson worked at the cannery from 1929 until it closed. At one time, he suffered a fall while working in the warehouse. Until he recovered completely, he was given the job of sitting in a giant replica of an Aylmer tomato juice can in front of the factory, selling tomato juice to passers-by at 5 cents a glass.

From 1958 until 1984, Canadian Canners had a branch on Walker's Line where cans were manufactured. This factory supplied nearly all of the company's requirements.

HYSLOP, David

In 1919, another canning factory came to town. It was the Ontario Canning Company which was located in Freeman,

Winning novelty relay team from Central Burlington School, 1932. K. Coleman, H. Lapington, G. Virtue, E. Henderson, J. Hyslop, E. Hodsdon. —*Courtesy Jean Hyslop Jarvis*

Central High School Jr. Basketball Team, 1930-31. —*Courtesy Jean Hyslop Ja*

close to the railway tracks. This company was owned by Dave Hyslop who, with his father, had operated a fruit plant in Greensville from which dried apples were sent to England.

The site at Freeman was selected because it was beside a railroad siding from which produce could easily be received and shipped. By 1925, the cannery was called Hyslop and Sons Ltd., but it later became Tip Top Canners Ltd., with plants in Burlington, Otterville and Greensville.

The Burlington plant produced canned tomatoes, tomato juice, peaches, pears and cranberries, as well as jams, jellies and marmalades. Mr. Hyslop was a "hands on" manager who spent a good deal of his time checking on the mechanics of production. His high production standards were matched by his high standards for the selection of the fruits and vegetables to be processed. Only the best for Tip Top!

David and Alma Hyslop and their six children lived in the fine old house called Maplelawn at 482 Burlington Avenue. This house had been built by George Blair, and featured an interesting octagonal tower. The home was the focal point for many happy social events. Alma Hyslop was active in the community with the Women's Association of Trinity United Church (now Wellington Square United Church), the Eastern Star, and the Burlington High School Board.

Jean Jarvis, one of the six Hyslop children, recalls attending school concerts in the small auditorium at Central Public School. She also remembers one county-wide field day in 1932 when the Burlington Central High relay team, each consisting of four boys and four girls, won all eight events! Since Mr. Hyslop had the first boat house behind the revetment wall at the foot of Burlington Avenue, back in the 1930s, the Hyslop family and their friends enjoyed boating, swimming and fishing.

Tip Top Canners Limited was sold to Stuart House in 1963 when Mr. Hyslop retired.

Tip Top can labels.
—*Courtesy Jean Hyslop Jar*

Tip Top Canners, 1926.   —*Courtesy Jean Hyslop Jar*

Harris Armstrong's gas station — Brant St. facing James St. This is the site of the present City Hall.
—*Courtesy Frank Armstrong*

rant St. looking South from Armstrong Bldg., 1953.
—*Courtesy Joseph Brant Museum, Frank Wright Collection*

Gasoline delivery.   —*Courtesy Joseph Brant Museum*

Cam Johnston in front of Johnston's Candy Store. Brant St. facing Elgin in 1922.
                                      —*Courtesy Jewel Johnsto*

Studebaker Agency — southeast corner Brant & Caroline Sts.　　　—*Courtesy Bill Cooke*

Hotel Raymond on Brant St. which is now the Coronation.

Playground at Indian Point, 1920.

—*Courtesy Brant Colema*

View from Brant Inn.

—*Courtesy Ross Tayl*

III

DEVELOPMENT

The very first developer in Burlington was Joseph Brant who, from time to time, sold off portions of his original land grant to settlers. As time went by, it was inevitable that the settlement would spread. Early developments such as Maple Avenue were spacious, farming neighbourhoods with gracious Victorian homes.

In the 20th century, development became more intense and compact until to-day we have a city with many commercial and residential areas. With to-day's rapid development, we often lose sight of the contribution made by the men whose foresight recognized the potential of the area surrounding the old town of Burlington.

COLEMAN, A.B.

Alfred B. Coleman was born in Woolwich, England in 1865, and came to Canada with his parents when he was still a boy. The family settled first in Hamilton, then came to Burlington.

At the age of 13, A.B., as he was known, worked on Mr. Bell's Lockhart Road farm for 50 cents a day. He was always interested in building, and as a young man taught himself to make and read blueprints. By the time he was 21, he owned the Ontario Street planing mill which later became Nicholson's. Soon, he was fulfilling his dream of building homes. In 1887, he built the large red brick house (now buff stucco) at 479 Nelson Avenue for his mother. A few years later, he constructed the "Gingerbread House" at 1375 Ontario Street across from St. Luke's church. This unusual building incorporates many interesting architectural features, and was featured in a short film about Victorian fretwork trim. Coleman lived in this house until 1899 when he sold it to Dr. Metherell of Hamilton.

By this time, Coleman was married to Samena DeWitt. In 1899, he purchased the Brant House property and built a huge modern hotel on the site. This was called the Brant Hotel, and immediately became the holiday resort of choice for many Canadians and Americans. Steamers came from Hamilton to dock in front of the hotel in Brant's Pond, bringing crowds of guests for picnics and day trips. A.S. Nicholson later told Brant Coleman that it was at one of these picnics that his father bought him the first banana he had ever seen. The poor lad ate the whole thing, skin and all!

As soon as the hotel was completed, the Coleman family moved to Toronto where A.B. was involved in several major building projects. In 1909, the family moved back to Burlington, taking up residence in the Annex, a building next to the hotel which had been built around the original Brant home. Around this time, Coleman purchased a small piece of property across the road on the lakefront and built a wooden building which he called his "country club". This was meant as a place for menfolk to gather to drink, smoke, play cards or billiards and otherwise socialize.

Meanwhile, A.B. began to develop the nearby Indian Point property at the mouth of Waghuata Creek, as the Indians called it, or Indian Creek as we know it now. First he made the Point accessible by building a road and a footbridge, then he laid out a six-hole golf course. Next he built several large bungalows which he rented to wealthy patrons. This later became an exclusive residential district, with attractive stone gates at each of the two entrances. However, A.B. retained ownership of the houses until his death in 1939. At that time, the estate sold the homes and gave the roads to the town of Burlington. For a long time, the streets were unnamed, but in 1951 members of the Coleman family chose names such as Algonquin, Iroquois, Indian and Mohawk for the streets.

When the federal government expropriated the Brant Hotel as a military hospital in 1917, Coleman turned his attention to his "country club". He expanded it into a first class hotel with fine dining and dancing. While Coleman was always interested in building, he was not interested in management. The Brant Hotel had always been managed by others;

Bowling Green at Brant Hotel.   *—Courtesy Ontario Archives S14713*

Sky Club, Brant Inn, 1936.   *—Courtesy Annie Smith James*

Gingerbread House built by
A.B. Coleman, Ontario St.

Friends on lawn at Lakehurst Villa, Lakeshore Road with the Flatts. The building was
demolished in 1992.   —*Courtesy Wynne Stewart*

so was the Brant Inn. In 1937, the managers were Murray Anderson and Clifford Kendall. When A.B. Coleman died in 1938, this team purchased the Brant Inn and turned it into one of the most famous night spots in North America.

For many years, A.B. Coleman spent the winter months in Palm Harbour, Florida. He could not resist working, even while on holiday, and was responsible for much of the early development in that city.

A.B. Coleman's interest in building was shared by his brother, Charles Findley Coleman. However, C.F. was not so much interested in the construction as in the interiors of buildings. He was a painter, paperhanger and interior decorator, in addition to his other occupations as a florist and a grain dealer. In 1890, he built the two-and-a-half storey clapboard house at 470 Nelson Avenue, probably with the help, or at least the advice, of his brothers A.B. and James H., since the latter was a carpenter and A.B.'s superintendent. In 1902, he built and lived in an attractive house on Elgin Street, looking down Nelson Avenue. Behind this home he had many hothouses where he grew violets, roses, carnations and chrysanthemums. In 1918, C.F. Coleman left his indelible mark on Burlington by being elected mayor. Always a progressive man, he had one of the first telephones in town. His telephone number was 5. Another of A.B's brothers, George, drowned in the Bay.

FLATT, W.D.

William Delos Flatt was undoubtedly the developer whose dreams and visions had the greatest impact on the tiny community of Burlington. He is remembered to-day through the names Flatt Road in Waterdown, and Flatt Avenue in Hamilton, but there are many less obvious tributes to his energy.

Born at Millgrove in 1862, W.D. Flatt was descended from a pioneer family of farmers and lumbermen. His great-uncle and grandfather, Robert Flatt, had come from the Orkney Islands as employees of the Hudson's Bay Company. On one occasion, the brothers were sent to escort a prisoner from the North-West to York (now Toronto). They walked over 1,000 miles, and for this service, the Flatt brothers were given a grant of 100 acres each on either side of the present Flatt Road, just north of Highway 403 off Waterdown Road. At one time, Flatt Road extended in a curve to the main street of Waterdown.

W.D. (or Willie, as his family called him) became interested in the lumber business at an early age, for his father owned a lumber company in Hamilton. When he was 16, he and his brother Jacob formed a partnership to export lumber from Michigan, Ohio and Quebec. This enterprise grew until it was employing 3,000 men during the manufacturing season.

In 1900, W.D. established the Trout Creek Stock Farm at Millgrove, and began importing thoroughbred Shorthorn cattle. On one trip abroad, he purchased a heifer, Cicily, from the Queen's herd, and became so well known that his cattle auctions drew buyers from all over North America.

In 1905, he became interested in real estate, and developed a large part of the southwest end of Hamilton, as well as the Brighton Beach and Buena Vista surveys on the north shore of the Bay in Aldershot. To enhance this area, Mr. Flatt encouraged the development of nearby Wabasso Park on the old Oaklands property. Wabasso is said to be an Indian word meaning "white rabbit". Flatt offered to improve the harbour at the park as his contribution to upgrading the area.

W.D. also saw the potential for development along the north shore of Lake Ontario, east of Burlington. In order for this development to take place, Flatt could see that a paved highway was necessary between Hamilton and Toronto. He promoted this project so vigorously that, in recognition of his efforts, he was presented with a loving cup by the Toronto-Hamilton Government Highway Commission on the completion of Highway 2.

To show his confidence in the development of the lakeshore area, in 1910 W.D. Flatt built Lakehurst Villa at 3074 Lakeshore Road. The stones for this fine house had come from Clarence Wood's farm on the Guelph Line. To provide water service for his home and the surrounding area, Mr. Flatt put in a watermain along Highway 2 from the Guelph Line to Shoreacres Road. Lakehurst Villa was purchased later by John Moodie, one of Hamilton's famous "five Johns" who formed the Hamilton Cataract Power, Light and Traction Company. In the 1930s, Mr. Moodie organized a ratepayers' association which purchased the water system and set up the Lakeshore Water Commission.

The Flatt family moved to Roseland Terrace, another luxury home in Port Nelson. As a member of Trinity United Church in Burlington, W.D. had organized a Sunday school in Port Nelson, and taught a class there for 15 years.

In 1912, Mr. Flatt published a promotional booklet describing the surveys he had laid out. Pine Cove Survey, between the Guelph Line and Pomona Avenue, offered choice lots with cement walks, electric light, telephone, post office and six acres of parkland. In addition, 600 feet of lake frontage was reserved for park, and a pier was constructed. Crystal Beach Survey at the foot of Walker's Line, Shore Acres at Appleby Line and Rose Hill Farm at the town line offered equally fine properties and the promise of an idyllic lifestyle. Lots ranged in price from $250 to $3,000. All surveys except Rose Hill Farm were served by the radial electric railway.

Flatt's dream was born before its time. Although the lakeshore did indeed offer luxury housing for the well off from both Hamilton and Toronto, it was many years before the area became as built up as he expected. Since he died in 1935, he did not live to see it.

Another of his dreams did come true. In 1885, Flatt had purchased a tract of virgin pine forest on Twelve Mile Creek in Kilbride. He thought this land would be ideal for recreation. However, he became engrossed in his many other projects and did nothing more about this land until 1924. At that time, he purchased the adjacent property which had been the site of the old Hamilton Powder Company plant, and built some rustic cabins which he sold as holiday homes to families from Ontario, New York and Pennsylvania. Within a few years, there were 78 such cabins, and the area was called Cedar Springs Community Club. The complex offered golf, swimming, and a community hall built on the site of the powder plant. During the winter months, the hills and wooded areas provided good skiing with an 8 foot ski jump and a rope tow.

When Mr. Flatt died, stone entrance gates were erected and dedicated as a memorial to this well-known developer.

For many years, George Brenholtz lived at Cedar Springs year round, serving as managing director and secretary of the Community Club. Those who skied at Cedar Springs in the 1940s and 50s will remember George opening the hall for them and lighting a fire in the huge stone fireplace so that skis could be warmed and waxed, and icy toes thawed out.

Daniel C. Flatt, W.D.'s brother, was also a lumberman who for some years was in partnership with his two brothers. In 1901, however, he became interested in scientific farming, and began operation of Summer Hill Stock Farm, a 233 acre tract adjoining his brother's Trout Creek Stock Farm. On this farm, he bred pedigree Yorkshire hogs and Holstein cattle which were greatly in demand throughout North America and Mexico. His show herds of hogs won every first prize at Toronto's Canadian National Exhibition for ten years in a row. They also won every first prize at the Chicago International Exhibition in 1914, and seven out of ten prizes at the Pan-American Exhibition at Buffalo. In 1907, Mr. Flatt formed the Hamilton Dairy Company which provided dairy products in the Hamilton area for over 50 years.

John Ira Flatt, father of William, Daniel and Jacob, had married Rachel Cummings of another pioneer family. In 1875, he was the owner of several mills and a large farm in East Flamborough. He served for many years on the Township Council, and eventually was elected Member of Parliament for that area.

In a sentimental volume published in 1916 by William Briggs of Toronto, W.D. Flatt told the story of his grandfather's arrival in Canada, and of his own life as a lumberman. The book, called *The Trail of Love*, reveals a man of great contrasts, from business acumen to deep introspection and love of nature.

VALLANCE, Mrs. Victor

At the turn of the century, May Elizabeth Moodie was a young girl, growing up in one of the prominent families in Hamilton. Her father, Col. John Moodie, was the founder of the Eagle Knitting Company. Also, as the owner of one of the first automobiles in Hamilton, a Winton, he was one of the founders of the Hamilton Automobile Club, the first of its kind in Canada. The family spent its summers at one of the pleasant houses on the beach strip, south of the canal.

May grew up in the social limelight. In 1912, she married Victor Vallance of another well-known Hamilton family. For the first 13 years of their marriage, the young couple lived in Winnipeg. By the time they returned to Hamilton, Col. Moodie had purchased W.D. Flatt's beautiful home, Lakehurst Villa, at 3074 Lakeshore Road. When Col. Moodie died, his daughter inherited the home. She lived there beginning in 1942.

While Mrs. Vallance lived at Lakehurst Villa, it was the scene of many large parties, many of them held for the benefit of Burlington organizations. For a number of years, the Burlington Garden Club held its rose show in the lovely gardens there. The Women's Auxiliary of Joseph Brant Memorial Hospital held a tea at Lakehurst, and Knox Presbyterian Church garden parties were also held there.

Mrs. Vallance kept many mementos of her illustrious father in the house. For example, there was a portrait of King George V with an inscription written by Queen Mary. For years, Col. Moodie had sent the royal family apples from the orchard on the Lakehurst property. The orchard later provided property for homes for two of Mrs. Vallance's children, George and Betty. In Col. Moodie's study was a model of the S.S. Turbinia. Col. Moodie and Timothy Eaton brought this ship to Canada from Newcastle-on-Tyne, and it was a familiar sight on Lake Ontario during the years when steamship travel was a convenient way of getting around on Lake Ontario. In the garage at Lakehurst, Mrs. Vallance kept the licence plates from Col. Moodie's cars, dating back to the turn of the century.

Lakehurst Villa was demolished early in 1992 to make way for several new homes. This was a great loss to Burlington's architectural and historic heritage. However, the properties on either side are still occupied by Mrs. Vallance's children who are a grandson and a granddaughter of Col. Moodie.

TOWNSEND, Thomas

The name Townsend is perpetuated in the annals of Burlington history through the name Townsend Avenue but Thomas Brooke Townsend should be remembered for a number of reasons.

He came to Canada in 1857, and the following year married Hannah Greening who was also an immigrant. As a civil engineer, he worked with the engineering department of the Great Western Railway. His first assignment was to rebuild the lower level bridge over the Desjardins Canal after the disastrous railway accident in which 60 people were killed. Later, he designed and built the special private railway car in which the Prince of Wales (later King Edward VII) travelled across Canada during his visit of 1860. He also designed the locks, gates and bridges for the Welland Canal which was being rebuilt at that time.

Townsend loved his work, but he also enjoyed farming on the property which he owned on Grindstone Creek, north of the railway line in Aldershot. His home there was called Wellington Cottage. In 1887, he devoted himself entirely to farming. Two years later when the nearby Oaklands property was offered for sale, he purchased 27 acres on the bayshore for $8,000. Eventually, he bought more of the adjoining property, dividing it into lots of a quarter acre or larger for gracious villa homes. The lots did not sell quickly, but they did pave the way for the later development of the central area of Aldershot.

The Oaklands property was originally owned by Lieutenant Alexander McDonnell who received a Crown grant of 2,000 acres in 1796. He sold 900 acres of this to William Applegarth who built a grist mill on Grindstone Creek in Hidden Valley in 1809. This "farm" part of the Oaklands property extended from LaSalle Park Road west to Daryl Drive and south to the bay. Applegarth built several homes on Oaklands, and over the years, a number of families occupied them.

Oaklands was purchased by Charles Davidson in 1872. He erected the gate house at the entrance to the estate, opposite Howard Road on Plains Road. John Fuller, son of the first

Anglican Bishop of Niagara, owned Oaklands next, and built yet another large house on it. Thomas B. Townsend bought the property in 1889 and it remained in his family until 1952. For many years, the main house at Oaklands Park was occupied by Emma Townsend and her nephew, Paul. The house had 26 rooms and was set in beautiful woods. John Fleming and his family lived in part of the house, and he and his wife were caretakers.

The gate house and houses were razed before the property was purchased by Jacob and William Cooke in 1956.

Part of the Oaklands property was acquired by the Hamilton Parks Board of Management in 1915 to become Wabasso Park. Canada Steamship Lines invested $150,000 in upgrading the park, and providing ferry services from Hamilton and the canal. The dock there had been a busy place for almost 75 years. Now it brought day-trippers to the amusement park which featured a picnic grove, 600 acre athletic fields, restaurant, a dance pavilion, and even a figure 8 roller coaster. There was also a fine cement bathhouse, since at that time the Bay was considered to be an excellent place for swimming. In fact, at one time there was a complaint that some swimmers were enjoying nude bathing! To protect the park's reputation, the Parks Board insisted that the last boat leave for Hamilton no later than 10.30 p.m. In 1923, the park was renamed in honour of the explorer Rene Robert Cavalier Sieur de La Salle who was said to have stopped there in 1669. LaSalle Park is still a popular recreation spot. The original pavilion remains, and the ruin of the bathhouse can be seen on the shore.

REIMER, Rudy

Nearly 200 years after the first settlers arrived, another young man reached Burlington via a similar route. He was destined to contribute a great deal towards Burlington's transformation from a small town into a progressive 20th century city.

Rudy Reimer emigrated to Canada with his parents just after the Second World War. The family was originally from the Ukraine, but had lived in Germany for eight years. They lived on a farm at Campden in the Niagara peninsula. During the summers, young Rudy picked fruit and thinned peaches on farms in the area. Then his parents decided to have a house built in Vineland. The builder, Bernard Epp, asked Rudy to work for him during the summer. Suddenly, the young man realized that this was an exciting business. He spent each evening poring over plans for the house, and for others that he helped build while working with Mr. Epp.

Eventually, he went into business for himself by taking a $5,000 mortgage on his parents' home and putting it into a credit union. He was thus able to borrow $10,000 from a bank to get started. He built 300 houses in Grimsby, then 15 in the Auchmar district on Hamilton mountain.

Making the move to Burlington was the result of coincidence. By 1961, land availability in Grimsby had dropped off due to lack of a sewer system, while new land was becoming available in Burlington. As it happened, six prospective home-buyers had indicated an interest in having homes built in Burlington, and they were all ready to start at the same time. Rudy Reimer therefore bought unsold lots from developer Gerry Stark and began building in Burlington. After the initial homes were completed, he built 500 more houses on the lakeshore, in Tyandaga Estates, and in the Ravenswood area.

About this time, the city of Burlington passed a by-law saying that residential builders must build a certain amount of commercial development as well, to help maintain a balanced tax base. Reimer therefore bought five acres of a business park on Mainway from the City. This was so successful that he decided to go out of residential building altogether.

His company purchased ten acres of Centennial Park on the Queen Elizabeth Way for commercial development. Later, 100 acres were purchased on Harvester Road, and development of this was completed in 1990. Another 80 acres on Burloak Drive are still in the process of being developed.

At one time, Reimer was on 18 different boards in Hamilton and Burlington, including the Burlington Chamber of Commerce, the Toronto Homebuilders Association, the Joseph Brant Memorial Hospital Board, and the Hamilton Philharmonic Orchestra. Not bad for an entrepreneur who arrived in Burlington with a $35,000 line of credit.

akehurst Villa from the front.   —Courtesy Hamilton Public Library

George Thorpe holding picture of Thorpe Homestead. Sears store is now here.
                                                  —Courtesy George Thorpe

Aerial view of proposed first industrial area, Progress Park, in 1968.

ROSART, John

Luigi Rosarti immigrated to Canada from L'Auquila, Italy in 1924. He settled in Hamilton where he met and married Lucy Cianconi. They raised seven children in the north end of the city. In 1944, Luigi died of pneumonia, just three months before he was eligible for his pension from the Steel Company of Canada. To provide the family with an income, Lucy had the idea of buying a neighbour's house, renovating it, and selling it for a profit. This worked so well, that Lucy repeated it again and again, moving her family into each house while it was undergoing renovations.

As a result of these experiences, her son, John, became fascinated by real estate and qualified as an agent. While still a young man, he arranged the sale of the Westdale Theatre in Hamilton, then assembled land for the Terminal Towers project in downtown Hamilton. In 1954, he had become successful enough to pay $10,000 for a bayshore lot on North Shore Boulevard, just west of King Road, where he built a comfortable home for his family.

In the early 1970s, John Rosart purchased several small market gardens at the intersection of Maple and Fairview Avenues, at a cost of $4 million. In 1984, he sold the 49 acre parcel that is now Mapleview Centre to Cambridge Shopping Centres for $14 million. He also sold the property east of Maple Avenue for the Maples subdivision. He and his family still own commercial properties in the Maple/Fairview area.

Rosart Properties Inc. was formed in 1975, and has interests in Fiesta Mall in Stoney Creek, Dundurn Place, and Stadium Mall in Hamilton, and the Canada Trust/Denninger plaza on Guelph Line, as well as properties in Simcoe and Niagara-on-the-Lake. John Rosart's brother, Domenic, and his sons Doug, Ken and John are all involved in the family's business enterprises.

In 1990, John Rosart and his wife, Anne, moved from their bayshore home on North Shore Boulevard to the renovated Hendrie/Cooper mansion across the street.

Mr. Norton's 'school bus': Irving Baker, Fred Bell, Don Peer, George Hamilton, Grant Norto
Marion Sherwood, Alfreda Martin, Betty Dolby, Evelyn Peer, Marie Ireland.

—*Courtesy Mrs. Mart*

Mr. W. C. Millward, standing, is the
Radial Railway Conductor.

—*Courtesy George Millward*

IV

MODERN TRANSPORTATION
COMES TO BURLINGTON

Burlington was catapulted into the Age of 20th Century Transportation in 1902 when Maxwell C. Smith brought the first motor car to town. It was a single cylinder Rambler, painted fire engine red. Soon everyone could identify the sound of its approach. Another early automobile was driven by Mr. Biggs, owner of the apple packing plant at Freeman. He was known as a very honorable man, and never drove faster than five miles an hour.

As the years rolled by, modes of transportation changed considerably, and other Burlington families made their mark in the field of transportation.

NORTON, Cecil

In 1936, the Cecil Norton family lived on Dundas Street, one-and-a-quarter miles west of Palermo. In September of that year, their son, Grant, was ready to attend Burlington Central High School. However, it was much too far to walk, and there was no public transportation. Cecil bought a seven-passenger Pierce-Arrow limousine in which he planned to drive Grant and some of his neighbourhood friends to school.

At times, there were 13 passengers packed into that vehicle. Students were asked to pay $3 a month, but those who couldn't afford to pay were never asked for money. Years later, when they were out in the work force, some of these students visited Mr. Norton to pay for the months when they had ridden with him. Some might never have gone to high school at all if it hadn't been for this transportation.

Before long, what had begun as a casual service had turned into a business. In 1946, Cecil Norton bought an old army chassis and fitted it with a bus body so that more students could be picked up and taken to school. The following year

Radial car. —*Courtesy Joseph Brant Museum*

Burlington Station. —*Courtesy Joseph Brant Museum*

Work crew building — railway line.   —*Courtesy Joseph Brant Museum*

Problem on the highway east of Burlington — Jack Wilson — 1923.
                              —*Courtesy Ann Smith Jones*

the school board began to pay for the bus service, so the Nortons purchased their first real bus – a Reo. By this time, Cecil had been joined in the business by his son, Grant, and his grandsons Alan, David and Michael.

The bus line was sold, first to Travelways, and then to Laidlaw Transit Limited. Alan Norton is now vice-president of the company's western region and is in charge of school and charter bus service for Burlington, Georgetown, Hamilton, Ancaster, Brantford and Paris. There are 680 routes with 68,000 students riding in 747 school vehicles.

An outstanding employee of the company was Mr. Gordon Alton, who, in 1990, received an award of distinction from Laidlaw Transit Ltd. for 35 years of safe driving. Mr. Alton had been driving students to school since 1954, covering about 1,400,000 kilometers. He began driving the school bus for Norton Bus Lines at a time when his dairy farm business was lagging. He can recall dropping children at the side of the Queen Elizabeth Way in the days before service roads.

The Norton family arrived in Burlington long before the motor vehicle. Alan Norton relates that his great-great-great-great grandmother Simmons was scalped by Indians while picking lettuce in her garden. Her husband also fell afoul of Indians. He was riding along an Indian trail, taking grain to be ground at the mill in Niagara Falls, when he was shot off his pony by Indians. Their daughter, Clarissa, was the first white child born in Halton County. She later told of picking wild cherries in what is now Gore Park in downtown Hamilton. Her husband, Francis Wilkinson owned a great deal of land. He traded 200 acres for a yoke of oxen; Goderich now stands on that land. Later, the 100 acre farm he traded for an Indian pony became the site of an Eaton's store in Toronto.

The family home, now more than 150 years old, had a room upstairs which had no windows and was reached by a trap door. Alan Norton believed that this room may have been intended as a retreat in case of attack by Indians. Considering the family's tragic experiences, this sort of precaution may have been a priority for early members.

Cecil Norton, founder of Norton Bus Lines, had many memories of the old Tansley bridge on Highway 5 near his home. The original bridge was at the bottom of the ravine, south of the present one. Old Model T Fords often had to be backed up the steep grade as the gas tanks worked by gravity. There was also a cable car over the ravine. This was supposed to be tied up on Sundays, but the young lads from the area knew how to unlock it, and they delighted in using it on that forbidden day. When the second bridge was built, the cement for the abutments was taken out on the cable car, and the steel girders were brought from Oakville.

It is a fitting tribute to Cecil Norton that when a new elementary school was opened in 1991 on Cleaver Avenue in Headon Forest, it was named C.H. Norton School.

HELDMAN, I.J.

When I.J. Heldman arrived in Burlington in 1911 to serve as station agent, rail service was provided by the Grand Trunk Railway.

The station was on Brant Street at Freeman. Until the 1880s, this busy settlement consisted of a hotel operated by the Baker family, a general store and post office operated by Mr. Cannom, a basket factory, a blacksmith shop and Biggs Apple Packing Plant.

The station agent had many duties. It was his responsibility to hire men to help him keep the station open 24 hours a day to sell tickets. They were expected also to send, receive and deliver telegrams; operate the gates from the watch-tower beside the tracks; and keep the station open for the arrival of many passenger trains. Mr. Heldman was also responsible for keeping in touch with the Beach Strip cottagers who leased their land from the railway. He constantly had to keep reminding them that they could not erect fences to keep people away from the lakefront.

As agent, Mr. Heldman also worked closely with Ted Smith (later a mayor of Burlington) who ran the express office. This was also a very busy place, especially during the fruit season from June to October.

Until 1912, there was also a railway station at the corner of Lakeshore Road and Maple Avenue. After it was closed, there was morning stage coach service that picked up passengers at the southern end of Brant Street and took them to the Freeman station where they could catch the train.

I. J. Heldman was born in New Hamburg, Ontario in the same house where Sir Adam Beck was born. When Mr. Heldman went to work for the Grand Trunk Railway, he was an agent in Norwich before being transferred to Burlington. In 1939, he was sent to Sarnia where he served until his retirement. For many years, while he lived in Burlington, he was treasurer of St. Luke's Anglican Church.

The railway station where Mr. Heldman worked for so many years was finally closed in 1988. At this time, the VIA Rail offices were moved to the GO station on Fairview Street. Joe Lipnicky who was station master from 1960 until 1985 said that a strong, cold wind would blow right through the old building. Nevertheless, it had been a favourite haunt for railway enthusiasts from all over the continent who often used to gather to watch the rolling stock.

V

COMMUNICATION, RECREATION AND THE ARTS

While business and politics play a vital role in any community, it is the lighter side of life that makes a city, town or village a worthwhile place to live. In Burlington, once the heavy work of pioneering was complete, citizens had the time and energy to devote to a wide variety of interests that not only enriched their own lives, but also made their town an exciting place. Early in the century, the town had groups for lawn bowling, hockey, baseball, lacrosse, yachting and almost every sport you can think of. The Musical Society, the Burlington Horticultural Society, the Burlington Boy Scout Association, and the Burlington Fine Arts Association provided stimulating activities with something for everyone. None of this would have been possible without the hard work of people like those who are remembered in this chapter.

SMITH, Spencer

During the last century, Thomas Barnardo, a young man with a reputation for being a bit of a ne'er-do-well, was so inspired by the plight of homeless street children in the east end of London that he acquired a medical degree and became one of England's early social workers. Eventually, he established 90 homes for destitute children. The children Dr. Barnardo rescued from the streets were given some schooling and religious education. The problem then became what to do with them.

Dr. Barnardo persuaded the Canadian government to allow the emigration of these children to Canada. At first, only boys came to work as farm help. Later, girls came also and worked as domestic helpers. Over a period of 57 years, more than 30,000 children were placed in Canada.

Rhoda Bell, Mary Bell, Lil Bell Smith, Spencer Smith.   —*Courtesy V. Gudge*

Spencer Smith Park.   —*Courtesy Mary Wright by Alex. J. Pe*

Closing in gaps to start filling in for
Spencer Smith Park.
—*Courtesy Jackie Crans*

Break Water
Burlington Ont.

he breakwater later became a park. Aerial view of Spencer Smith Park before filling in.
—*Courtesy Ontario Archives - AD638*

One of these was Spencer George Smith who came from England in 1885, at the age of 15. His widowed mother had no means of supporting Spencer and his sister, and was forced to allow them to leave home. Upon his arrival in Hamilton with a group of Barnardo boys, he met Fred Martindale of Caledonia who hired him for a year. In a touching poem called Reminiscences, written when he was 41, Spencer Smith told of the kindness of Mrs. Martindale to a lonely boy, and how her influence remained with him throughout his life.

Later, Spencer went to work on the Bell family farm on Maple Avenue in Burlington. He later married Edith Bell, the daughter of his employer. After a brief sojourn in Toronto where the Smiths ran a store, they returned to Burlington to open a grocery store on Brant Street. The high quality of his fresh produce attracted a large clientele, including passengers from pleasure boats on Lake Ontario who docked at Burlington for the express purpose of shopping at Spencer Smith's store. It is said that when children came into his store, they were always given a treat. Perhaps the kind, gentle Mr. Smith was remembering his own beginnings as a Barnardo boy.

For 35 years, Spencer Smith was an active member of the Burlington Horticultural Society, and was responsible for the planting of many trees on Burlington streets. During the Depression, he hired striking cannery workers to clean up the shoreline at the foot of Brant Street. This was the beginning of Spencer Smith Park. He spent a great deal of time working on the park himself, and enlisted the help of volunteers. For example, he sometimes asked Harold McGrath, owner of a local transportation company, to deliver another load of stone or top soil for the park. This was delivered by Brock Harris or one of Mr. McGrath's other employees. Mr. Smith obtained plants for the park from greenhouse operators, while the first willow trees were cuttings which he took himself from trees in the garden of Dorothy Angus, Burlington's chief librarian. Some of them are still flourishing!

In 1947, the town of Burlington presented Spencer Smith with a silver tray to honour him for his tireless efforts to make Burlington a more beautiful place. The Ontario Horticultural

REMINISCENCES
                    by Spencer Smith

'Twas six and twenty years ago,
   And perhaps a little bit more,
When I, a lad of fifteen years,
   Lit on this fair Canadian Shore.

Fate led the way to Hamilton,
   And there a man I met,
Who said a likely boy to do the chores
   I certainly must get.

I don't think I looked likely;
   For the voyage had been rough,
And leaving home and friends behind,
   I felt most mighty tough.

But the farmer thought I'd suit him,
   If I'd try and do what's fair:
So we came to an agreement,
   And I hired for a year.

We boarded the train at King street -
   I'll never forget that day;
It was in the spring of eighty-five,
   On the twenty-first of May.

My thoughts were busy all the way,
   On the new life I was now to begin;
To me the prospect seemed gloomy,
   And my future loomed very dim.

We arrived at Caledonia.
   And the farmer's old bay mare
Soon took us down the river road
   To the farm, six miles from there.

The buggy we rode in was classy,
   The roads none I'd seen could compare -
We took so much on the wheels as we went
   It's a wonder there's any now there.

My boy courage rose as I entered the house,
   And I saw the farmer's wife.
I'll never forget her as long as I live;
   And bless her all my life.

I had my tea and went to bed,
   And slept as sound as a trout.
And the first thing I heard in the morning
   Was: "Come, boys, it's time to get out."

I put in that day in a hazy way;
   For a lonesome boy was I,
And as I drove the cows to the fields
   I heaved many a deep, deep sigh.

Each day was filled with surprises,
   And, Oh, the mistakes I did make!
Were the things I broke put together
   They'd be worth all the wages I'd take.

The farmer was often impatient;
   And often discouraged was I,
But one thing that kept up my courage
   Was the farmer's good wife and her pie.

The cows and the horses, the sheep and the pigs,
   Were ever a worry and care;
But since I have left them I think of them still,
   And in my dreams fancy I'm there.

The lessons I learned on the farm are worth more
   To me than mere dollars and cents;
And if I were privileged to start over again,
   It's life on the farm I'd commence.

The farmer's wife has gone to her rest,
   But her influence lives in me still:-
She helped lift the load along life's rough road,
   And save me a start up the hill.

                    Spencer Smith

* The farmer's wife was
        Mrs. Fred Martindale

Monument to Spencer Smith.
                    —Courtesy George Hawley

"Reminiscences" by Spencer Smith.

Society rewarded him with a gold medal in recognition of his outstanding contribution to the community.

When he retired in 1950, he devoted himself to the development of a small park on the waterfront at the foot of Brant Street. At that time, there was a narrow strip of grass along the steep cliff on Lakeshore Road. At the bottom of the cliff was a strip of water, protected by the breakwater, and used for anchoring small boats.

In 1964, the area behind the breakwater was filled in, and the park extended to Locust Street, thus covering a total of 13 acres. Toronto landscape architect J. Austin Floyd was hired to prepare a master plan for the entire park. In 1967, Spencer Smith Park was further developed to reach all the way to the old Brant Inn site, and a new seawall was built along the shore. The area at the foot of Brant Street was developed under Centennial Year grants. Some thought the name of the park should be changed at this time, but the Burlington Historical Society put up strong opposition, and Spencer Smith is still honoured to-day in the park's name. A plaque on the upper pathway at the park is dedicated to his memory.

Each year, the park is the scene of two huge arts and crafts shows which draw exhibitors and visitors from far and near. It is also the site of the Sound of Music Festival held in June.

When Spencer Smith died in 1955, he was a highly esteemed resident of Burlington. If Dr. Barnardo had been alive , he would have pointed with pride to the success of one of his boys.

BRANCH, Laurie

For 21 years, Laurie Branch was known in Burlington as "Mr. Recreation". He guided the town and later the city's recreation program through its busiest and most progressive years.

Until recreation became structured in the 20th century, Burlingtonians enjoyed simple sports such as ice skating on ponds and outdoor rinks, swimming in the lake, toboganning and roller skating on the paved streets.

Later, there were organized clubs and teams. In 1904, Burlington had several lawn bowling clubs. One of them was opposite Trinity Methodist Church on Elizabeth Street, while others were located in Central Park, on Shadeland Avenue and in Roseland. In 1912, the town was proud of its championship hockey club. The first swimming pool was built in the 1930s at Hidden Valley Park. When the radial line was abandoned, the Lion's Club purchased the site of the car barns, and this became Lion's Park.

In 1946, the Province of Ontario established grants for communities to form recreation commissions. This was done in Burlington in 1950, with Ted Lambert as the first director. Since then, recreation facilities have proliferated. In the early 1960s, statistics showed that Burlington had the highest rate of participation in arts and crafts for all of Halton and Peel.

A native of Fort Erie, Laurie Branch came to Burlington in 1967 as director of recreation services. Soon after his arrival, he was approached by the Burlington Musical Society which was at a low ebb. Ted Smith of the Society asked Laurie Branch if he would be interested in having the music society come under the Recreation and Parks Department. This was done, and beginning almost at once, all musical programs were under Mr. Branch's direction. This included the Teen Tour Band which had been organized in 1946 by Elgin Corlett. This well-known band now tours the continent. Burlington has the largest municipal music program in Canada.

Laurie Branch was also involved in the organization of the Burlington International Games which began in 1968. At the request of town council Mr. Branch prepared a list of cities and towns in North America with the name Burlington. There were 23. Burlington, Vermont was the second largest of these (Burlington, Ontario being the largest). Mr. Branch got in touch with his counterpart there and suggested an athletic exchange program. The Burlington International Games are still held annually, alternating between the two cities.

In 1980, Laurie Branch established the Sound of Music Festival which was patterned after the Waterloo Music Festival he remembered from his youth. The festival's name was suggested by Mrs. Branch.

HARRIS, Elgin

Elgin Harris arrived in Burlington in 1899. He was a graduate of a Hamilton business college, and had worked as a printer's devil at the *Grand River Sachem* in Caledonia, as well as at the *Hamilton Spectator* and newspapers in Wingham and Petrolia. Now he was ready to buy his own newspaper, the *Burlington Gazette*, which had been faltering and was in the hands of the bailiff. For $1,500 he was able to purchase the list of 300 subscribers and the equipment.

At first, the office was a tiny space in a building on the south side of Water Street. When this property was purchased for the canning factory, the newspaper was moved to Elgin Street. Alas! the Elgin Street site was needed for a power line, so the newspaper moved once again, this time to 370 Brant Street where it remained for many years.

Because of his concern about Burlington's water supply, Harris ran for the office of reeve and was elected for the 1921-22 term of office. The following year, he became mayor. His son, George, also took an interest in local politics, serving as councillor, reeve, and from 1936 to 1939, mayor.

Elgin Harris was editor and publisher of *The Gazette* until his retirement in 1956. His son, George, and then his nephew, Richard, had worked with him. On his retirement, the newspaper was sold to a group of Burlington businessmen. Elgin Harris died in 1975 at the age of 99.

Marjorie Harris, Elgin's daughter, recalled that her great grandfather was Richard Cole who came to Wellington Square in 1853, working first as a carpenter and wagon-maker. Later, he bought the bake shop on Water Street (Lakeshore) at the corner of John where the old bus terminal was located. The family lived over the bake shop. His daughter, Mary Jane (Marjorie Harris's grandmother) took leftovers from the bake shop to Nelson to give to the Indians who worked on the local farms.

SINGLETON, Roy

When Roy Singleton came to Canada from England in 1960, he planned to get a job as a navigations officer on a Great Lakes freighter. A graduate of the Merchant Naval Academy,

Elgin Harris.
—Courtesy Joseph Brant Museum

Roy Singleton.   —Courtesy The Post

View of lower Brant St., showing LePatourel Drug Store.

—Courtesy Hamilton Public Library

Mary LePatourel, later Homer, Tom LePatourel and Daisy in front of their home decorated for Edward VII.

he had served at sea, and planned to continue his career on the inland waterways. However, when he married shortly after arriving, he decided that it would be more practical to seek a career that would not take him away from home for most of the year.

He went to work at the *Oakville Beaver*. When the newspaper's owners decided to start a sister publication in Burlington, Roy Singleton was hired as ad manager. The *Burlington Post* began operations in a small office at the corner of Caroline and John Streets. The first issue hit the streets on September 15th, 1965. Two years later, the newspaper was purchased by Inland Publishing, and in 1970, Mr. Singleton was named publisher.

Under his guidance, *The Post* graduated from its status as a weekly newspaper. In 1980, a Saturday edition was added. Since February, 1986, it has been published each Wednesday, Friday and Sunday.

Like his newspaper, Roy Singleton has become an integral part of the community. He has been actively involved with the Burlington Figure Skating Club, the Burlington International Games, the Burlington Visitor and Convention Centre and many other local groups.

LePATOUREL, Tom

The first telephone conversation in history took place on March 10th, 1876 between Alexander Graham Bell and his assistant, Thomas Watson. Before long, people all over the continent were talking to each other by means of this amazing new invention. It was not long before the telephone reached Burlington.

In 1880, Tom LePatourel, whose forebears had come from Guernsey Island, bought the drug store on the east side of Brant Street near Pine. The business had catered only to the summer trade, but Mr. LePatourel turned it into a year-round operation. When the Bell Telephone came to Burlington, he was designated the company's agent for the village. The switchboard was installed in the dispensing room at the rear of his drugstore. At first, Mr. LePatourel handled all the calls himself, providing service on week days from 8 a.m. to 9 p.m., and on

Brant St. at the Lake — Baxter & Galloway Mill.

Ship at Baxter's Wharf.

View of cannery from wharf.

Street scene showing sidewalks & street lamps.
—*Photos by Mrs. LePatourel, Courtesy John Homer, grandson*

Sundays from 2 to 4 p.m. The first three subscribers, in addition to the drugstore itself, were Kerns and Co., Messrs. Baxter and Galloway, and Freeman Brothers.

In 1890, Mr. LePatourel was a member of the first class to graduate from the Ontario College of Pharmacy. Later, Tom's daughter, Marion (Daisy) also graduated from the Ontario College of Pharmacy, and eventually became the owner of LePatourel's Drug Store.

In 1900, subscribers requested 24 hour service, but had to wait until their number reached 100 before Bell would comply. Tom's brother, E.J. LePatourel, was sent out from the Hamilton office to canvass the town for the additional subscribers required. He managed to obtain 20 more, and the 24 hour service was established. Rates were $15 a year which included three free calls a day to Hamilton.

When he built a new building for his business on the east side of Brant Street, next to the bank at the corner of Brant and Water Streets, Tom LePatourel made extra space for the switchboard which was then operated by Pansy Anderson. Mr. LePatourel remained as Bell Telephone agent in Burlington until 1914. The Bell Telephone office stayed in the drugstore until 1925 when larger quarters were found elsewhere on Brant Street.

When the dial system was installed in Burlington in 1949, Marion LePatourel was invited to make the first local call, an honour that her father would have appreciated. Immediately after this, the first long distance call from Burlington was made by Mayor Norman Craig.

One of Daisy LePatourel's part-time employees was her great-nephew, John Homer who worked in the store while he was attending school. In 1978, when the LePatourel family home was caught in development on Elizabeth Street, John decided to move the 1854 building to its present site on Malvern Road. The old house was not just the family home, but had historic value because it was built for Alexander Chisholm, a member of one of Burlington's pioneer families. The LePatourels would have applauded John Homer's efforts on behalf of their beloved family home.

ROBERTSON, William

In 1945, William Robertson was reeve of Nelson township. He had a dream of a park on Twelve Mile Creek at Lowville. With the assistance of Paul Fisher and A.S. Nicholson, he arranged for the purchase of the Featherstone farm. Because the land was covered with thick hawthorn bushes, it took 56 men and 11 tractors a whole day to clear the land. The men then worked for weeks to clean out the creek and build a steel bridge, a refreshment stand and a ball diamond. On the day of the official opening, Mr. Robertson pulled the switch to light the area for the first time.

Mr. Robertson had farmed for many years on Walker's Line. He was elected to the township council in 1934, serving first as councillor, then as deputy reeve, and finally as reeve. From 1946 until amalgamation in 1958, he was sheriff of Halton County. His contribution to the development of Lowville Park is still being appreciated by the people of the Burlington area.

HUNT, Cliff

Growing up in a Salvation Army family gave Cliff Hunt a close association with music from an early age. He took piano and cornet lessons, and later studied music with Dr. Graham Godfrey, organist at Melrose United Church in Hamilton.

Cliff Hunt was working as a foreman in the die shop at Greening Wire when the R.C.A.F. asked him to be cornet soloist in the Air Force Band. He accepted, and later went on to become the youngest conductor in the Royal Canadian Air Force during the Second World War. He spent 29 years with the air force, retiring with the rank of wing commander. In 1951, he brought his family to Burlington to live.

Since beginning his musical career, Cliff Hunt has conducted the Ottawa Symphony Orchestra, the U.S. Navy Band, the Caribinieri police band of Rome, the NORAD band and the Canadian bomber group band. After retiring from the air force, he ran the grandstand entertainment at the Canadian National Exhibition for 14 years, bringing to that show such varied performers as Alice Cooper, the Red Army Chorus, Anne Murray and the Mormon Tabernacle Choir.

Col. Cliff Hunt, of the Burlington Concert Band.

Burlington and District Junior Community Boys' and Girls' Band. Elgin G. Corlet
Director, 1949.   —Courtesy Daryl Fitzner, Photo by Lloyd Bloo.

In 1992, Mr. Hunt is still involved with music on the home front. He has been a member of the Sound of Music Festival committee, and directs the Burlington Concert Band. In 1990, his achievements brought honour to the city when he was awarded a silver medal by the Louis Sudler Foundation of Chicago.

CORLETT, Elgin

Burlington is known all over the continent, and even abroad, because of its widely-travelled Teen Tour Band for young people. For almost 45 years, enthusiastic boys and girls have been putting on excellent musical performances that are a credit to the city.

It was through the efforts of councillor Frank Ellerbeck that, in 1947, his cousin Elgin Corlett was invited to come to Burlington to form a young people's band. The town had had a number of bands for adults over the years, but never before had youngsters been invited to take part. What began as an experiment became an integral part of Burlington's heritage.

Elgin Corlett was on a stopover in Hamilton while travelling with a circus when his cousin asked him to come to Burlington. When he arrived in town, over 200 young musicians signed up for music lessons and a chance to be in the band. Mr. Corlett remembered one lad who rode his bicycle up to the practice hall and asked for the bandmaster. When Corlett replied that he was speaking to him, the boy said, "But I expected an old, white-haired man!" "Just give me time!", ho was told.

In spite of his youthful appearance, Elgin Corlett had had plenty of musical experience before coming to Burlington. As a 12-year-old, he studied saxophone, trumpet and clarinet, and began to play with the Leamington Citizens' Band. After graduating from high school, he played with a dance band which toured Ontario and Quebec. In 1939, Mr. Corlett enrolled at the Dana Musical Institute in Warren, Ohio. For three years, he was assistant to his brother, Charles F. Corlett who was supervisor of music at Warren G. Harding High School in Warren. He also played in Canadian Army bands and shows overseas during World War Two.

When the Corlett family moved to Burlington, Elgin took the position of music supervisor at Hillfield College in Hamilton, and was also director of music of the Lorne Scots Militia Unit in Georgetown.

At first, the new youth band was called the Burlington and District Junior Community Band. Under the sponsorship of the Chamber of Commerce, the Burlington Musical Society was formed. Through the Society, school students were encouraged to register for music instruction. Aptitude tests were given, and those who qualified were given lessons. Mr. Corlett provided the students with the music, and with instruments from his own collection of clarinets, saxophones, drums, trombones and trumpets.

The band's first out-of-town trip was to parade with the band from Warren G. Harding High School at the Cleveland Bowl Stadium. The Warren, Ohio band then came to march with the Burlington band in the Warrior's Day parade at the Canadian National Exhibition. The exchange continued for many years. The Burlington band later became known from coast to coast when it participated in Gimbel's Thanksgiving Day parade in Philadelphia, the Rose Bowl parade at Pasadena, California, and at the Orange Bowl and Disneyworld in Florida. In 1984, the band marched on a beach in France with the 25th Canadian Brigade in a special D-Day anniversary ceremony.

After amalgamation in 1958, the band was renamed the Burlington Teen's Tour Band. This was later revised to Burlington Teen Tour Band. For the first eleven years, the band practised in a room over Ellerbeck's store on John Street. When the music centre was built in Central Park in 1964, the band practised there or in the Lions Club Hall, and held drill marching rehearsals in the adjacent park. Elgin Corlett himself trained majorettes to accompany the band, one of the original ones being his daughter, Carol Ann. Garnet Corlett took an active interest in her husband's band, going along as chaperone on out-of-town bus trips.

In view of his contribution to Burlington's cultural image, it is not surprising that Elgin Corlett has been referred to often as "Mr. Music"!

BATEMAN, Robert

Many people are not aware that the famous artist, Robert Bateman, lived in Burlington, and influenced many young people during the years that he taught art at city high schools. While living here, his beautiful home on the escarpment provided just the right setting to inspire his artistic talents.

A native of Forest Hill, Ontario, Robert Bateman is a naturalist, conservationist, and sportsman. All of these influence his work on the canvas. At the age of 12, he joined the Junior Field Naturalists Club at the Royal Ontario Museum and became an enthusiastic bird-watcher. At the same time, he enjoyed painting, so it was natural for him to combine his two interests. After graduating from the University of Toronto with a degree in geography, he travelled extensively throughout Canada, as well as in Europe and Africa. He spent two years teaching in Nigeria, then returned to Canada to live in Burlington.

At first, Mr. Bateman taught art and geography at Nelson High School, but before long he was devoting his entire time to teaching art at Lord Elgin High School. By the mid-1970s, his paintings were so much in demand that he gave up teaching. For a year, he continued his association with the Halton Board of Education as art consultant.

PECK (Slavin), Alice

The Peck family purchased the home at 2100 Lakeshore Road in 1959. It is an 1843 farmhouse, originally of board and batten construction, which had been bricked over in the late 19th century. In June of 1960, Alice Peck opened The Treasury of Canadian Handcrafts shop in the two rooms at the front of the house.

The following year, an art gallery was built onto the west end of the house, extending the front facade. This was opened in November, 1961 as the Alice Peck Gallery. With the opening of this gallery, the Burlington Public Library, then located on Elizabeth Street, discontinued its art shows. Librarian Dorothy Angus used the extra space to enlarge the children's department.

Alice Peck Slavin in her craft shop. —Courtesy *The Post*

First & Second Port Nelson Girl Guide Companies, 1948.
—Courtesy *Jackie Crans, Photo by Arnold Wilbur*

Sea Cadets on Brant St., around 1950.   —*Courtesy George Hawley*

Burlington Hockey Champions, 1912.   —*Courtesy Joseph Brant Museum*

Burlington Lacrosse Team, around 1912.   —*Courtesy Ivan Cleaver*

Aldershot Baseball club, winners of inter-county league & Wilson Cup. R.D. Smiley, Frank Easterbrook, Walter Filman, Nat Benton, Bang Gadow, Harold Emery, W. Easterbrook, Sam Job, Wm. Scheer, R.H. Emery, Wm. Filman, W.A. Emery, J. Smiley, Holby, Jas. Filman, H. Paine. —*Courtesy Joseph Brant Museum*

The first artist to show in the new gallery was Sylvia Singer-Weininger, a McGill Art graduate who then lived in Burlington. Other local artists who exhibited were Gery Puley, a teacher of water colours; Kathleen Cardiff, printmaker and batik artist; and Gerard Brender à Brandis, wood-engraver and bookwright. In 1962, Alice Peck established the custom of having at least one craft-artist exhibition each year, and one group show for new artists who were usually local.

Robert Bateman's first one-man show was held at the Gallery during Centennial Year, 1967. All the paintings were of Halton County, and it was the first sell-out show for the Gallery. While teaching in Burlington, Robert Bateman inspired and encouraged many young artists. Of these, Deborah Pearce, Leigh Cockburn, E. Rob Ross, Chris Bacon and Alan Barnard all had shows at the Alice Peck Gallery.

Burlington craftspeople who have exhibited included Barbara Irvine, potter and painter and her son, Steven Irvine, who is now a Master Potter; Frances Forstner, weaver who founded the Burlington Weavers Guild; Winnifred Laking of the Rug Hooking Guild; Anne Gallagher, potter and glassmaker; Gene Drummond, silversmith; Faye Rooke, R.C.A., internationally known enamelist; and Denise McKay, painter and porcelain artist.

In 1978, an upstairs gallery was added. During the Gallery's 20th anniversary year, two special events took place. One was a second show of work by Robert Bateman. The other was the Gallery's first juried award show which was won by Betty Goodfellow, who taught art at Lord Elgin High School.

The Alice Peck Gallery closed in 1987. The building now houses real estate and medical offices.

HUME, Rex

Burlington's first motion picture theatre was the Crystal on Brant Street, opposite Ontario Street. The proprietor was Rex Hume, a native of Milton who was descended from a pioneer family in the Scotch Block. Lyle Tuck was the projectionist for many years. Rex Hume and his family lived on Emerald Crescent.

When the Crystal burned in 1930, Mr. Hume purchased a site for a new theatre on Water Street (Lakeshore Road) near Brant Street. For many years, this property had housed Dr. Watson's office, and a baby clinic. The clinic was moved to the basement of the library on Brant Street to make way for the new theatre complex, for Mr. Hume built not only a modern theatre with all the latest sound equipment, but included in the building space for a store on either side of the theatre, and offices and apartments upstairs.

Jackie Crans recalled in recent years that, as a child, she and her friends attended the Saturday matinees. Admission was 12 cents, and the program included a cartoon and a newsreel, as well as the feature attraction. Occasionally, when a friend had no money, a chum inside the theatre would quietly open the exit door to admit him or her.

The new movie theatre was named the Hume. It later became the Roxy, then the Odeon. The building is still being used commercially, but the theatre is gone. Recently, Christopher's Restaurant, on the site of the original Brant Street theatre, was destroyed by fire.

Ruins of the bathhouse at LaSalle Park.
—*Courtesy Dorothy Turcotte, Photo by A.J. Hannaford*

Parade on Lakeshore at Brant St. at installation of King Edward VII Memorial Fountain & Horse Trough, 1912. Now at City Hall.   —*Courtesy Ontario Archives S14710*

Sons of England Float.   —*Courtesy Ontario Archives S14711*

St. Matthews Anglican Church, Plains Road in 1900.

VI

BURLINGTON CHURCHES

To the early settlers, religious beliefs were a vital form of sustenance. Often isolated, the pioneers craved the association and expression that their church connections provided. They met whenever possible, and built small churches as soon as the size and affluence of the congregation warranted it. Even into the 20th century, the spiritual and social benefits of church attendance continued to be of great importance. Residents of the area put as much of themselves and their income as possible into the maintenance of their churches. The variety and depth of their beliefs created a rich background fabric for the rest of community achievements.

In the late 1950s and 1960s, Burlington experienced a spate of church building. During this period of unprecedented church expansion, the new congregations included Strathcona Presbyterian, Glad Tidings Assembly, St. Raphael's Roman Catholic, Holy Cross Lutheran, Prince of Peace Lutheran, Burlington Alliance, St. Elizabeth's Anglican, St. Stephen's United, St. Gabriel's Roman Catholic, St. Philip's Anglican and Port Nelson United Churches.

WYATT, Henry

The land on which St. Matthew's Anglican Church, Aldershot, stands was originally Crown land. In the early 1840s, it was purchased by Henry Wyatt who had emigrated from Surrey, England. Henry and his family attended services at St. Luke's in Burlington, but often wished that there were a church nearer home.

In 1849, they began to solicit money for this purpose. The first donation came from Lord Bayning. Later, Mrs. Wyatt's brother-in-law, Matthew Card, made several donations to the fund. A piece of land on Plains Road was donated by the Wyatts, and in 1860, stone was purchased for the foundation and lumber was obtained for the window frames. Work began in 1861. The wooden church building was constructed by Samuel West at the cost of $158. The fence cost an additional $2.

The first service was held on September 22nd, 1861, the day after St. Matthew's Day. This fact, plus the fact that Matthew Card had contributed generously to the building fund, gave the church its name, although for some time it was often referred to as Wyatt's Chapel of Ease.

The Rev. Thomas Greene of St. Luke's conducted the first service. At first, the rector of the new parish was the Rev. J. McKenzie of St. John's Church (later All Saints), Hamilton; then from 1865, St. Matthew's was in the charge of the Rev. C.H. Drinkwater of St. Thomas', Hamilton. Over the years, many clergy were responsible for St. Matthew's before the parish had its own minister.

In 1915, the church building was raised and set on a foundation, all the work being done by volunteers. During this period, an old parishioner once recalled, there were rows of tile piled up outside the building. One Sunday evening, a parishioner came to the service in a rather inebriated condition. Afterwards, a friend met him at the front door to see him home safely. As they walked by the tiles, the inebriated one kept repeating "third row, fifth tile". When they came to the third row, he reached into the fifth tile and retrieved a bottle of whiskey which he had placed there before entering the church!

Henry Wyatt had built his family a fine farmhouse on his property. It is believed that he first built a small house, then added to it until it became an eleven room home. Apparently nothing was too good for Henry Wyatt's home, for he imported the glass windows from England.

Herberton House, named for Henry Wyatt's grandson Herbert Marsh, has been restored and lovingly cared for by its 20th century owners, and can still be seen at 164 Townsend Avenue East. Woodwork in the house is similar to that of Dundurn Castle, and was carved by hand. The floors are made of pine boards two-and-a-half inches thick which probably came from the Wyatt property. Moulding and trim throughout is yellow pine. The house is said to be haunted by a friendly ghost who walks through the front hall into the kitchen, every night at 8 o'clock. Perhaps it is Henry Wyatt, checking to see that his house is being well cared for.

VYSE, James

When Edna Vyse was a little girl, she and her parents attended St. Matthew-on-the-Plains Anglican church in Aldershot. At that time, the church was a very small building with no basement. Consequently, it was very hot in summer, and very cold in winter, even with the pot-bellied stove well stoked. The Sunday service was at 3 p.m., preceded by Sunday School at 2. George Sinclair would come at 2 to light the stove, ready for the arrival of the adults. Meanwhile, the children suffered the cold during their lessons.

On Saturdays, Mr. and Mrs. Sinclair would enlist the help of Edna and some of their own daughters to clean the church ready for the Sunday service. Flowers on the altar were usually from someone's garden, although at Christmas, Alfred Read donated red carnations. After the church was raised and a basement added, it was a delight for the children to watch the flutter of the ladies' garments as the choir proceeded over the furnace grate in the aisle.

Sometimes heavy snowstorms prevented church attendance. There were no snowploughs, so everyone had to stay indoors until the men of the village could dig through the drifts. Many social events associated with St. Matthew's were held at Herberton House which at that time was owned by the Reads. Edna Vyse was proud that for the harvest festival services her father provided the tallest corn to decorate the church.

The Vyse family came from England in 1913. James Vyse came first, in April of that year. He went immediately to Aldershot where he found good friends in the Townsends at Oaklands Park. They rented a house to him, and helped him to decorate it, ready for the arrival of his wife and daughter. When James applied for his first job at National Fire-Proofing Company, he presented himself dressed in his best suit, and carrying a walking stick. He asked for an outside job, since he had suffered ill health after working in a smoky area of northern England. The superintendent at the factory told him to report for work the following day, but to come dressed in dark overalls. James walked to Waterdown to buy the necessary outfit at Egan's store. His first job was digging clay, but he was later discovered to be skilled with machinery, and became a millwright.

Meanwhile, Lilian Vyse became impatient in England. In May, she booked passage for herself and Edna on the Empress of Ireland. In writing to tell her husband that they were on their way to Canada, she forgot to tell him the name of the ship. This was fortunate, as it turned out, for there was a dreadful storm, and the Empress of Ireland was reported lost at sea. The ship arrived safely, although many days late. When Lilian and Edna arrived at the Stuart Street railway station in Hamilton, it was midnight. The station master was closing up, and since they could not get to Aldershot that night, he locked them in until morning. The next day, when they took the train again, the conductor told them that they had to get off at Waterdown. Lilian Vyse was upset, for she did not know that the Aldershot station was called "Waterdown". The newcomers had to trudge around Aldershot asking for James, and they were very weary by the time they found him. Lilian was so appalled by the condition of their new home that she vowed she would go straight back to England. However, she stayed, and soon came to love Canada.

Later, the family rented Valley Farm from the Hendries. While living there, Edna met Syd Wickens. She just thought of him as a friend until he went away. Then suddenly, love blossomed. The couple was married at St. Matthew's in October, 1928, with the entire village invited to attend. The church was decorated with flowers from friends' gardens, and the food was catered by Lloyd's of Hamilton.

It was a heartbreak for the many who loved the picturesque little church when it was razed in 1966 to make way for a larger, modern building.

STOKES, Dr. S.B.

When the Rev. Dr. Sidney B. Stokes became rector of West Plains United Church, he was inheriting a historic parish and planning a brand new building.

The first West Plains church had been built in 1878. It was a one-room white board and batten building with rounded windows. The building cost $400 and was built on land donated by William Hendrie, adjacent to the Royal Botanical Gardens. At that time, Plains Road was a rural thoroughfare with lush market gardens on both sides. The original parish roll consisted of about 90 people.

However, when Dr. Stokes was rector, the present Gothic style stone and brick church was built by the increasingly prosperous parish. Dr. Stokes and his wife, Elva, had to work hard because he was also the minister for East Plains church, a mile or two down the road. In addition to this, Dr. Stokes was chaplain for the town's senior citizens.

Additions to the church were completed in 1962 and 1968, providing space for Christian education and administration as the parish continued to expand.

When West Plains United Church celebrated the 60th anniversary of its building in June, 1990, Dr. Stokes was celebrating his 100th birthday. This provided a double occasion for a special service and luncheon, with Dr. Stokes as guest of honour.

TEBBS, Rev. G.W.

Officially, he was the Rev. G.W. Tebbs, rector of St. Luke's Anglican Church in Burlington, but to many, he was "Old Man Sunshine".

This colorful clergyman was the shepherd of the St. Luke's flock from 1919 to 1942. Everyone within range of radio station CKOC had heard of him, however, for his regular broadcasts were popular with many outside of Burlington, and outside of the Anglican Church.

George W. Tebbs was born in Peterborough, England, and received his university education there before coming to Canada. He attended Wycliffe College in Toronto, and was ordained priest at Christ Church Cathedral, Hamilton in Feb-

St. Luke's Anglican Church.   *—Courtesy Hamilton Public Libra*

"Old Man Sunshine" CKOC Radio's "The Sunshine Club", around 1935 — Minister, St. Luke's Anglican Church.

ruary, 1913. He served at parishes in Hamilton and Orangeville before coming to Burlington. He was appointed to St. Luke's after the untimely death of the previous incumbent, the Rev. Frank Hovey, who died of influenza at the age of 39.

St. Luke's was fortunate to have a man of such great character and diverse interests. Mr. Tebbs arranged for the mortgaging of the rectory so that the property next door to the church could be purchased. A building fund was established to which the rector gave the first contribution as a thanksgiving for the safe return of his son from the war. As a result, the new parish hall in memory of those who died in the First World War was built in 1922 at a cost of $24,300. Mr. Tebbs' energy was boundless. He was active in the Boy Scout movement and was a school trustee as well as being a founding member of the Burlington Lions Club. To serve Anglicans in the east end of Burlington, he established a mission church at Strathcona School with Edmund Holtby, layreader, in charge.

After the First World War, the Town wanted to erect a monument in honour of those who fought. Elgin Harris of *The Gazette*, Aleck Leitch of the canning company, Hughes Cleaver, and Mr. Tebbs all gave money to pay for the monument. Mr. Tebbs insisted that the best place for the monument was in the waterfront park, opposite the grove of trees leading from the lake to the front door of St. Luke's. The monument stood there for many years before being moved to a site beside the city hall.

But George Tebbs was best known for his role as "Old Man Sunshine". It is said that he owned the first radio set in Burlington. The ladies of the Women's Auxiliary enjoyed their weekly meetings at the rectory, for it gave them an opportunity to put on the headphones and listen to the rector's radio for a few minutes. Certainly Mr. Tebbs could see the value of radio, for he presided at the first religious service ever broadcast in Canada. Beginning in 1922 he arranged to have St. Luke's services aired regularly over CKOC. Then in 1931, Herb Slack, a Burlington resident who owned CKOC in Hamilton, had the idea of a series of programs designed to bring cheer into the lives of listeners who were suffering from the Depression. He wrote three scripts and asked George Tebbs to read them over the radio, using the name "Old Man Sunshine". The series was so popular that it continued for 11 years. During that time, Mr. Tebbs travelled daily to and from Hamilton, and received thousands of letters from listeners. Before his retirement, he had made 3,000 broadcasts.

Mr. Tebbs also carried on a tradition set by the first incumbent at St. Luke's. He loved gardening, and visitors often dropped by to see the irises and other flowers that grew so abundantly in his garden. In 1919, he revived the Burlington Horticultural Society and became its president. At its first meeting, the organization agreed to beautify the town with trees, flowers and shrubs, and to promote the rose as the town's official flower.

When St. Luke's celebrated its 100th anniversary in 1934, Mr. Tebbs organized a number of events. On the avenue leading up to the church from the lakeshore, 44 new trees were planted to replace those which had not survived the century since Mrs. Thomas Greene laid out the avenue. A garden party was held at the home of Mr. and Mrs. Edmund Holtby who lived at the foot of the avenue, with the party overflowing onto the open space itself. In October, special thanksgiving services were held. At the grand finale on October 28th, the order of service was taken from a prayer book dating back to the time of Queen Anne. Guest speaker was the Rev. H.S. Snell of the Mohawk Institute, Brantford, who brought, for St. Luke's use on that occasion, a set of communion plate presented to Joseph Brant's grandfather by Queen Anne in 1712. The pieces were buried for safety during the American Revolution, then brought to "Her Majesty's Church of the Mohawks" (Mohawk Chapel in Brantford) when it was built in the 1790s.

During the Second World War, Burlington was honoured to have a minesweeper named after the town. When the 180-foot ship was commissioned and dedicated in September, 1941, the ceremony took place at Spencer Smith Park, with Mr. Tebbs officiating. More than 1,500 people turned out to see the ship arrive. After the war, the ship was scrapped, but the bell was salvaged. It was lost for many years, but is now on display outside the Iron Duke Sea Cadet Hall at Elizabeth and James Streets.

Although always a very popular and amiable man, Mr. Tebbs could be outspoken when the occasion warranted. On New Year's Day, 1936, he pointed out that while thousands of couples had danced at local "pleasure spots" to see in the New Year, less than 50 had been able to attend the watch-night service at St. Luke's. "I stood here New Year's Eve," he is quoted as saying, "and felt like praying God to send another depression.

"Are we again to live in days like those when hundreds of thousands of men went money-mad? Must we again sow the wind, only to reap the whirlwind, and at the expense of mind, of soul and spirit?"

One can't help but feel that Elizabeth Brant Kerr, St. Luke's early benefactress, would have found a kindred spirit in Mr. Tebbs, for they were both well-known for their vivacity, sense of humour, forthrightness and good nature.

BRIDGMAN, Burwell

One of the earliest families to settle in the northern part of Nelson Township was the Bridgmans who arrived in 1813. The family has always been prominent in the village of Zimmerman which once thrived in the hollow where Twelve Mile Creek crosses Appleby Line.

Like many pioneer families, the Bridgmans were staunch Methodists. Salem Church, one of five originally within driving distance of Zimmerman, was built on land donated by the Bridgman family. It stood on Walker's Line at No. 2 Sideroad until 1905 when it was purchased by the residents of Kilbride, and moved to their village for use as the community hall.

In the 1870s, many Methodist circuits held annual camp meetings which provided an opportunity for prayer, praise and fellowship. Salem camp meetings were held at Burwell Bridgman's farm. The meetings took place in late summer, and usually lasted from Thursday to Thursday. People came from miles around to enjoy a wholesome holiday, socialize with old friends, and renew their spiritual commitment. Some brought their own tents, while others rented them at $3.50 or $6, depending on the size of the tent. Good pasturage was provided, and horses could be fed for 25 cents a day.

At that time, many splinter groups were breaking away from the Wesleyan Methodist church. One of these was the New Connexion. It was hoped that camp meetings would help reunite these splinter groups. Apparently it was successful. New Connexion advertised the Salem camp meetings in its publication, *Evangelical Witness*, and eventually the Wesleyan and New Connexion congregations were reunited. Salem church then joined with nearby Bethesda to become the Zimmerman Methodist Church in 1882. At first, services were held in an abandoned school which was also used for boxing matches. This association did not appeal to the Methodists, who were glad to build their own church. Burwell Bridgman was in charge of the building committee, and the new brick church was completed in 1891 at a cost of $2,900. The old building, now Trinity Baptist Church, has one stained glass window which was erected by Marion Sybil Bennett, (a Conservative M.P. from 1953 to 1956) in honour of the early pioneer Bennetts.

During this period, Zimmerman was a busy little village. Named after the family who settled the valley, the village at one time boasted a general store, two sawmills, a grist mill, a shoe shop, a tailor shop, a carpenter, a blacksmith, a school and a post office.

In 1911, the grist mill operated by the Crawford family burned down and was not rebuilt. It remained derelict until the 1920s when a Mr. Van Fleet bought it and rebuilt part of the mill on the original foundation. Once again, grain was ground for the local trade. However, this did not last long. For a while, the property was leased for a Toronto Fresh Air Camp, with the new building used as a dormitory. Later, Mr. Nixon of Tansley bought the building and moved it away. In 1928, Frances Jones of Toronto bought the property and renovated the original house and grounds as a guest house for the elderly. She also bought the adjoining store and ran it successfully as a grocery and gift shop. Upon her death in 1939, the property was sold, and the building finally torn down.

This was the end of Zimmerman, the village that was established to serve the farming and lumbering community of the previous century.

Another thriving community which had an early Methodist connection was Port Nelson. In the mid-19th century, Guelph Line was a busy street, often crowded with grain and farm wagons taking produce to be shipped from the dock on the lakefront. In 1873, the villages of Port Nelson and Wellington Square amalgamated to become the village of Burlington. Yet both communities were still mainly rural. Port Nelson remained a farming neighbourhood until the mid-20th century.

The first place of worship in the village was the Wesleyan Methodist Chapel build in 1862 on the Guelph Line near Water Street. This white frame building is now the headquarters of the Burlington branch of the Canadian Red Cross.

In 1952, a group of Port Nelson area United Church members, under the aegis of a Trinity United Church committee, reopened the old chapel for church services. Soon, however, a site for a new church building was dedicated at the corner of Rossmore Boulevard and South Drive. The cornerstone of Port Nelson United Church was laid in 1961. One noteworthy contribution made by the Port Nelson congregation to Burlington was the impetus it gave to the local Inter Church Council to help establish a counselling service for local citizens (COHR) which provides individual and marriage counselling, as well as educational programs for family life and marriage preparation.

A Methodist Society had been formed by Wellington Square residents in 1852. They met in various locations before erecting their first church on the corner of Elizabeth and James Streets in 1858. This is now the Sea Cadet Hall. Later, another Methodist church was built on the north side of the town hall. In 1925, the Methodists, some of the Presbyterians, and the Congregationalists joined forces to create the United Church of Canada. Burlington Methodist Church then became Trinity United Church. In 1965, the congregations of Trinity United and St. Paul's United built Wellington Square United Church on Caroline Street.

OGG, Nelson

Roman Catholics living in Burlington did not have their own church until 1861. However, the parish of St. John the Baptist was established in 1849, with the Rev. John Cassidy coming from Dundas to celebrate Mass once a month. He also travelled to Waterdown, Milton and Oakville. Those who wished to attend services more frequently had to travel to St. Augustine's in Dundas.

Until the church was built, the faithful gathered at the home of Nelson Ogg on Pine Street. When it was decided that a church should finally be built, Ogg donated land at the corner of Pine and Pearl Streets. This early church had no floor, and only boards for pews. It was a mission church until 1925 when the Rev. D.A. Ford became its first full-time pastor. St. John's Church on Brant Street was built in 1952, four years after the construction of St. John's Separate School on the adjoining property.

Nelson and Joseph Ogg came to Ontario from Quebec. Nelson settled in Kilbride before moving to Burlington around 1851. He and his wife, Lucy, had 12 children, and later moved from the Pine Street house to the two storey brick house at the northeast corner of Brant Street and Blairholm. Nelson is listed in directories of the period as a cooper, so it is not surprising that his son, Joseph N. Ogg operated a cooperage and harness building. Napoleon, Joseph's brother, was also a cooper and lived on Pine Street, where the Village Square is now. Later, Joseph N. Ogg ran a livery stable at the corner of Water (Lakeshore) and Locust Streets. After retiring, he continued to work as a cooper in a shed at the rear of his Pine Street home. The barrels he produced were always quickly sold.

J.N. Ogg served on council for many years. During his tenure, the radial railway secured its franchise to come to Burlington. A rate of five cents, one way, was agreed upon, but representatives of the company did not want it specified in the by-law. Eventually, the by-law was worded to allow a maximum return fare of 25 cents. This remained in force until 1919, when it was changed to 35 cents.

As Burlington's oldest citizen, Mr. Ogg planted a tree in front of the public library as part of the Confederation celebration in 1927. It is recorded that the tree did not live, but Mr. Ogg went on until 1936 when he died at the age of 96.

In 1896, George Blair purchased Nelson Ogg's 50 acre farm on Brant Street. The house, Blairholm, is still standing, and at the time of writing is occupied by Stanley Blair, George's son. Stanley recalls that his father built an addition to the house soon after purchasing the farm because Mrs. Blair wanted a larger kitchen.

Another of Nelson Ogg's sons who contributed to the development of Burlington was Perulin N. Ogg who, in 1894 was a commissioner of the fire department. In that year, council decided to erect a bell at the town hall. This bell was to be rung in case of fire or other emergency.

Minutes of fire commission meetings reveal that in 1897, Mr. Ogg moved that the Burlington Fire Commission purchase four coats, six pairs of boots, six hats, five pairs of gloves, one pole hook with chain attached, one roof ladder, one fire ladder, one lamp and table for the fire hall, one four-foot steel bar, all to be obtained for the cheapest prices possible. As it turned out, the boots, coats and hats were purchased for a total of $26.40.

Joseph Ogg, Nelson's brother, came to Burlington around 1861. He and his wife, Adele, had six children.

Two other Oggs who appear in the records were James and William, both coopers as well, but apparently supporters of the Presbyterian church.

HASTINGS, Morris

Mary Ruff grew up in the village of Freeman, living with her parents and two brothers in a home on Plains Road opposite the present site of Holland Motors. Some of her mother's relatives, the Armstrongs, operated the general store and post office in the village. Her father, Ulrich, who had come from Germany worked on the "peeler" in the basket factory at Freeman. Later, he went to work for the CNR where he earned $45 every two weeks during the Depression.

Mary remembers life in Freeman during that era. For example, she bathed in a big tub, brought into the kitchen just for that purpose. The house was heated with a coal oil stove in the basement. Another stove was used on the main floor during the winter, being set up in the fall and removed in spring. Potatoes and carrots were stored for the winter in a pit dug in the ground. Mary's parents worked together to make sauerkraut and head cheese.

Like other children from Freeman, Mary attended Burlington Central School when John Lockhart was principal. The students took their lunches to school, and in inclement weather, ate them in the school basement without supervision! While attending Burlington Central High School, Mary attended parties at the home of a friend who lived at 360 Torrance Street, now the site of an apartment building. The home belonged to F.W. Watson, local coal merchant and mayor of Burlington in 1934-35.

Mary graduated from St. Joseph's School of Nursing. Then, in 1934, she married Morris Hastings who worked at Nicholson Lumber and later became manager there. The couple lived on Pine Street, and attended St. John's Catholic Church at the corner of Pine and Pearl Streets, where the Ukrainian Catholic Church of Holy Protection stands to-day. When the first board of trustees was chosen to build a separate school, Morris Hastings was elected. Land on Brant Street had been purchased from William Bell for this purpose, and St. John's School was built in 1948. A few years later, the Hastings became aware of the need for more local accommodation for teachers at the school, so they added three apartments to their home for that purpose. Eventually, their property was sold for the Village Square development.

Mary had attended the original St. John's Church as a child. At that time, it lacked both heat and electricity. A neighbour had to provide water when it was required, and look after the key. When the present St. John's Church was built on Brant Street in 1953, Morris Hastings was chairman of the building committee.

One of the outstanding priests at St. John's was Father Daniel Ford. When he first came to Burlington, he lived on Brant Street, but later his uncle bought him a house on Water Street near Smith Avenue, paying $10,000 in cash. One of Father Ford's best friends in town was Mr. Tebbs at St. Luke's

Anglican Church. After serving the Burlington congregation for 20 years, Father Ford moved to Elmira before retiring to St. Joseph's Villa in Dundas. He died in 1976.

COULSON, Edwin

When Ella Gunby married Edwin Coulson at the turn of the century, the young couple moved into the Colling family home on the Guelph Line near the corner of Britannia Road. At that time, the house was only about 15 years old, and had been built as a companion to the Methodist parsonage on the corner next door, although on a smaller scale.

The Coulsons' 8 children were born and grew up there. The first seven children were born in the big bedroom down-stairs, but the youngest son, Howard, was born in the parlor. His mother made him four winter dresses from the skirt of her creamy wool cashmere wedding dress which had been saved for some special use.

The Coulsons were a very close-knit family, and all of them were together at the table for all meals, including break-fast. The family was very much involved with Lowville United Church. There was an active Ladies' Aid Society with about 35 members. Each member paid ten cents a month, and in return was kept busy baking, quilting and sewing.

There is a legend that early this century, a Hallowe'en prank was perpetrated at the church, and no one has yet solved the mystery of how it was accomplished. On the morning after Hallowe'en, passers-by were amazed to see astride the ridge pole of the church a lumber wagon fully loaded with bags of grain! Later, the wagon disappeared as mysteriously as it had appeared.

In the 1920s, Mrs. Coulson purchased a new Brussels carpet. At the time, the minister at the parsonage was known for his eagerness to ask the price of things. Mrs. Coulson was determined not to tell him the price of her new carpet. Nevertheless, she asked him in to see it. He knelt down to feel it and turn over the corner, then turned and said, "If you wouldn't think me too saucy, how much . . ." to which Mrs. Coulson replied, "Oh, step on it, Mr. C., step on it and see how soft it is on the feet!"

Eleanor (Ella) Coulson & Edwin
(Eddie) on Golden Anniversary,
1950.   —Courtesy Irma Coulson

Josiah Lambshead & Mary Jane Partridge
Lambshead in 1921. The first Sunday
School picnic of Freeman Mission at
Bronte Beach.   —Courtesy Elsie Ghent

At about the same time, during renovations, a bathroom was added to the house. It was the first in the village, and Aunt Sarah Colling warned that too much bathing would be injurious to the children's health. Her gloomy prediction did not come true, for the children suffered only the usual childhood communicable diseases. The only tragedy occurred when Kenneth, age 15, was involved in a bobsleigh accident and died as a result of his injury.

The family home, still occupied by Coulsons, is a ten-room brick centre hall plan home with gables and walled dormer windows with trilobular Gothic detail.

LAMBSHEAD, Josiah

Early in this century, Josiah and Mary Jane Lambshead lived on the south side of Plains Road at King Road, near Campbell's Corners. Their little brick house was called Half-and-Three-Quarters because it was built into the side of a hill, and had an upstairs bedroom that was lower than the rest of the rooms on that floor. There are now apartment buildings where this little house stood. Josiah was a market gardener who grew celery, raspberries, currants, wine cherries, sweet cherries and sour cherries on his farm. Indian Creek ran through the property, and was used to irrigate the crops.

Josiah and Mary Jane had seven children. When they grew up, these children married into well-known local families such as the Tregunnos, the Almases, the Cannoms, the Ghents and the Lindleys. When their son, Albert (known as Net) married Ethel Job, Josiah and Mary Jane gave him a piece of land facing King Road where he built a house. Albert was an elder of East Plains Methodist Church. After hearing an evangelist speak, he felt The Call, and accepted the Lord as his Saviour. On this same occasion, his parents and his sister, Ruth, were also saved. Albert approached the minister at East Plains church to ask if they could hold prayer meetings in the church. Not wanting to favour or offend any group, the minister said "no", and so the meetings were held in Josiah's home. Others joined the group, and in time it was decided that a larger meeting place was needed.

In 1921, Mary Jane Lambshead, then widowed, and her daughter Lillian obtained a small house on Plains Road and called it the Freeman Mission. It was to serve "north Burlington" which, at that time, was the area around Freeman. Net Lambshead was the first pastor. Later, the congregation moved to a building on Brant Street, opposite the old Freeman House (now the Henry Seiders' funeral parlour). Mrs. George Pollard had saved her money from skinning onions and bought the property for $1,000 to give to the church. Contractor Hugh Reid supervised the men of the congregation who did most of the work. Mr. Morse did the masonry on the attractive red brick building. Freeman Gospel Tabernacle was opened in 1928. Later, the name was changed to Brant Street Bible Church, but when a new building was erected on Highway 5, it became known simply as Brant Bible Church.

As president of Associated Gospel Churches, Net Lambshead travelled to western Canada to encourage the gospel churches there to join the Ontario association. Many did, and while out west, Net ordained a number of ministers. Also as a result of the efforts of Net Lambshead and the Freeman gospel church, Fairhavens, a conference centre in the north, and Cama (Christian and Missionary Alliance) Woodlands Nursing Home on Panin Road in Burlington were established.

A train passed the Freeman intersection every six minutes, and four trains a day carried mail. Consequently, the postal service was excellent. Net could write in the morning to a friend in Toronto, and receive a reply that same evening. At the railway crossing, there was a water tower, and also another tower which the gateman climbed so that he could see to operate the crossing gates.

The Lambsheads knew the Freeman settlement intimately. Net's daughter, Ethel Davy, recalls that William Cannom had the store and post office there. Mr. Cannom, who had previously operated a grocery store in Hamilton near the market, had married Ina Ghent of Burlington. They had two daughters, Thalia and Sybille. Mr. Cannom's sister married a Lambshead, thus giving him close connections with two well-known Burlington families.

Deborah Jane Emory Easterbrook, Ella Joan Easterbrook Job, Ethel Thompson Job Lambshead, Ethel Mary Lambshead Lemon, Davy, 1915. —*Courtesy Elsie Ghent*

The Freeman House, a high-class boarding house, had its name painted in large letters on the side of the building. Ethel remembers going there with her Uncle Walter when he took fruit to the station, and being given 25 cents to buy ice cream cones at the Freeman House ice cream parlor.

After Josiah Lambshead died, Mary Jane and her daughter, Lillian, moved into a house on Maple Avenue. At that time, there were four Lambshead houses in a row. There is now a street called Lambshead Drive in this area.

Net's sister, Lillian, was a great favourite with her many nieces and nephews. She was a very short person, and each child considered it a red-letter day when he or she became taller than Auntie Lil. Often, she would give the children small loaves of bread to take home to their mothers. On one occasion, Ethel Davy recalls that she had a tea party by herself with the bread, instead of taking it home. Later, she was called upon to account for the missing loaf!

One of Josiah and Mary's children died tragically. Frederick was a young lad when, on Christmas Eve, the candle he was carrying upstairs to bed set fire to his nightgown.

Two of Net Lambshead's daughters became missionaries in Africa. Ruth, a nurse, devoted herself for many years to work in Malawi. Ethel Davy married Clayton Lemon in 1937. After he died of chronic nephritis in 1953, she became a missionary in Kenya. In keeping with the family tradition, Ethel's daughter, Muriel Jane Weber, taught at a Christian school in Puerto Rico.

DE BRUIN, Hubert

After the Second World War, many Dutch families decided to come to Canada to make a better life. One of these was the DeBruin family who arrived in the Burlington area in 1951. Hubert De Bruin had owned a florist business in a village on the outskirts of Rotterdam. He, his wife and six children aged from 1 to 13 intended to settle in the Holland Marsh area, but a friend in Hamilton offered to take them under his wing. Within a day of arrival, Hubert De Bruin had found work at the Unsworth greenhouses in Aldershot. The family moved into a cottage on the property.

The early years in Canada are remembered as being very happy, with a sense of togetherness shared with the neighbours. Hubert planted his own garden which grew so abundantly that vegetables were traded for other commodities. The neighbours' Christmas gifts are especially remembered, for these included ice skates with boots, a great novelty since the children had previously only owned the old-fashioned clamp-on skates.

The family attended the Canadian Reformed Church in Hamilton. Hubert's weekly wages were $20 of which $2.50 was set aside for church collection.

When Mr. DeBruin left Unsworth's, it was to start his own business in painting and glazing greenhouses. Soon, he had his own greenhouses as well on Dynes Road. All of his children grew up to have successful business or professional careers.

Hubert DeBruin became well-known in the Dutch community as a fieldman for the Immigration Committee of the Canadian Dutch Reformed Church. In this volunteer capacity, he found jobs and living accommodation for Dutch immigrants arriving in Canada. Most of the new arrivals were willing to take any kind of job to get started. One father of ten said he would be willing to clean septic tanks.

Soon after his arrival, Mr. DeBruin became one of the founders of the Ebenezer Canadian Dutch Reformed Church. At first, services were held in the old arena on New Street, then in Glenwood School, and still later at the Sea Cadet Hall. In 1955, a church was built on Dynes Road. This fine building was destroyed by fire in 1989. At first, it was feared that all of the records for the Canadian Reformed Church across Canada had been lost in the fire, but fortunately they were recovered in satisfactory condition. The church was replaced by a larger building opened in 1990. John Calvin School had been built earlier on the church property as well.

Burlington also has another Dutch church, the Christian Reformed Church on New Street which was built in 1959. In 1964 this congregation started the Trinity Christian School on Walker's Line. At this school and at John Calvin Christian School, the students receive religious instruction as well as

Knox Presbyterian Church, 1910.   —*Courtesy Joseph Brant Museum*

George Blair, born 1852, died 1935.—*Courtesy Isobal McKeen*

academic education based on the Ontario elementary school curriculum.

BENT, James

In the 1850s, the few Regular Baptists of Wellington Square met at the home of James Cushie Bent at 507 Elizabeth Street. In 1875, the trustees for this group bought the property at the southwest corner of Ontario and Locust Streets. Here the Gothic style church, now known as St. Philippe's French Catholic Church, was built by Mr. Bent, a master builder. It was known as Calvary Baptist Church.

After the Second World War, a group of local Baptists from the Convention of Ontario and Quebec started a new Baptist congregation. In 1954, this group built Burlington Baptist Church at Bridgman and New Streets.

BLAIR, George

George Blair became a member of Knox Presbyterian Church when he married and moved to Wellington Square from Kilbride. From that time until his death, he kept the church in good repair. George's sons Stanley (now 102 years old) and John (now 97) and several other members of the Blair family are still faithful members of Knox Presbyterian Church.

In 1923, the Rev. Russell McGillvary became minister of Knox. At a meeting the following year, the congregation met to decide whether or not they would enter the union of the Presbyterian, Methodist and Congregational Churches. On January 10th, 1925, it was announced that the majority had voted to join the union. The name of Knox Presbyterian Church was changed to Christ's Church of the United Church of Canada. Those who had voted against the union were invited to join the new congregation or to use the church building on Sunday afternoons. They chose to do neither, meeting at St. Luke's Parish Hall instead.

Because of a technicality, the next year an amendment was passed allowing a second vote. This time, the union was defeated. The Rev. McGillvary vacated the chair, leaving the keys and records behind. Divine services were resumed in the Knox Church building, with large crowds in attendance.

Elders elected included George Blair and Edwin Peart. These events caused hard feelings between those who chose to join the United Church and those who continued as Presbyterians. Some of these are still felt among the older generation. Both denominations, however, went on to become healthy entities, thus fulfilling their purposes in Burlington's growing community.

Rev. Sidney Stokes of West Plains Church. He was the First Minister of the new church dedicated in 1930, and is now Emeritus Minister.

Calvary Baptist Church on the corner of Locust & Ontario Sts. It is now St. Phillipe Church.
—*Courtesy George Hawley*

Miss Edith Donkin, Strathcona School.
—Courtesy Phyllis Brandor

Strathcona School.

—Courtesy Phyllis Brandc

VII

SERVICES TO THE PUBLIC

Although the first residents of the area lived very spartan lives, and were engrossed in the daily struggle for survival, they were very aware of the importance of the intangible aspects of life. As soon as possible, they organized schools so that their children could pursue an education. Churches to nurture the soul were also a top priority. Most of the first families took an active part in the organization of one or both of these institutions. It wasn't until later that there was time or resources to provide a hospital, a library, a volunteer fire department and other public services. When the right time came, however, there were plenty of volunteers anxious to see that excellent facilities were established.

TRILLER, Philip

Burlington Central School got its start in December of 1859 when a Mr. Triller donated an acre of land to the trustees of School Section No. 1 of Nelson Township. A two storey school house was built on the site. It was constructed of red pressed brick from Milton, ordered through Phil Patriarche's Brant Street business.

By 1906, there was a definite need in Burlington for secondary education. Burlington students who wanted to go to high school had to travel to Hamilton, with the result that many dropped out after Grade 8. So it was decided to add two classrooms to Central School to provide space for high school classes. That fall, 34 students were enrolled in the high school program. By 1911, it was clear that the old building was not adequate for the needs of the growing community.

The following year, an eight-roomed school replaced the old building at a cost of $33,000. Students from kindergarten to graduation continued to study together until 1922 when a separate high school was finally built.

Mr. Triller's contribution to education in Burlington is still in evidence. The Trillers were an interesting family who were among the earliest settlers in the area. In 1888, when he was 88 years old, John Triller Howell wrote about his family's early years, first in Grimsby, then in Trafalgar. His maternal grandfather, Philip Triller and his two sons came from New Jersey to join his wife's family in Canada. They spent a year at Grimsby where John Green told the men that if they would build a dam for him, he would allow them to saw all the lumber they needed at his sawmill. When the work was completed, they rafted the lumber from Forty Mile Creek to Twelve Mile Creek where the Trillers settled. Subsequently, Philip Triller owned 1,000 acres of land between Burlington and Bronte. Lakeshore Road in Bronte is shown on early maps as Triller Street, and the old Bronte public school was known as Centriller.

DONKIN, Edith

When Burlington was still a town, people settled down and remained in the same career niche for many years. Such was the case with Edith Donkin who, for 40 years, served at Strathcona School.

In 1913, the first Board of Trustees had their eye on a site in W.L. Smith's apple orchard as the ideal spot for a school, and with that in mind, they purchased two acres of land. Soon, a red brick schoolhouse was built on Walker's Line. The building had one classroom and a teacher's room on the ground floor. When the school opened in September, 1914, there were 29 pupils.

The trustees, W.D. Flatt, J.T. Tuck and Colin Smith, had no trouble choosing the name for the new school. The nearby community hall was called Strathcona Hall because a donation had been solicited from and generously made by Lord Strathcona. W.L. Smith called his property Strathcona Orchards, so the school became Strathcona Public School. By 1921, enrollment had reached 63, so a two-roomed addition was built. Soon after, Strathcona became the first school in the county to include home economics and manual training in its curriculum. With the opening of the Strathcona and

Ravenswood housing developments in the 1950s and 1960s, a four-roomed south wing and a north wing with library, auditorium and classrooms were added.

In 1924, Edith Donkin joined the teaching staff after graduating from Hamilton Normal School. It at once became clear that Miss Donkin was an exceptional teacher. She taught the first home economics and industrial arts courses, and established auxiliary classes for children who needed special assistance. Many of her music and arts students excelled. In 1951, and again in 1954, Strathcona students won first prizes in the urban school competition for murals at the Canadian National Exhibition. School choirs, under her direction, won a number of cups and shields at the Halton Music Festivals.

It is not surprising that her many achievements earned her the position of principal which she retained from 1943 until her retirement in 1964.

Edith Donkin's sister, Kathleen, also played an important role in education in Burlington. She taught for a total of 38 years at Lakeshore and Burlington Central Public Schools. At the latter, she set up the first home economics class, and taught it until her retirement.

In June, 1988, Strathcona School was closed due to low enrollment. Pupils were transferred to John T. Tuck School where the newly renovated library/resource centre was named the Strathcona Library. Many artifacts from Strathcona School, including the original corner stone and Edith Donkin's portrait were transferred to the library. Strathcona School was demolished, and a number of expensive homes now occupy the site.

The Donkins had been well-known in Burlington for many years. Edward Donkin had come from Ponteland, Northumberland, England around the turn of the century. In 1910, Mr. Donkin, always a lover of children and everything youthful, presented local reporters with samples of his new creation, a stick candy called "Burlington Rock". The reporters duly wrote about the high quality of the candy, but there is no record that it made a great impression in the candy industry. For the last 15 years of his life, Edward Donkin wrote a weekly

Apple orchards at Strathcona School.

—Courtesy Phyllis Brandon

S.S. #14 Nelson in 1940, Maple Ave. & Plains Rd. Annette Huffman, teacher.

—Courtesy Irma Coulson, Annette Huffman Marsha

column in the *Burlington Gazette* under the pen name "Uncle Tim".

PATTINSON, Helen

Until modern development obliterated it, the Maple Avenue community was a close-knit and happy one. The families who lived on Maple Avenue, and nearby on Plains Road were the Davidsons, the Lambsheads, the Almases, the Williams, the Banks, the Thorpes, the Lindleys, the Pearts, the Smales and many others. Each beautifully kept home had a lovely garden. And there were many children.

On Plains Road just opposite Maple Avenue was the school that these children attended. It was S.S. No. 14, also known as Plains School or "Miss Pattinson's School". The two storey brick building was constructed by George Blair at a cost of $2,050. It stood in a large yard with plenty of trees.

Helen Pattinson was born in Milton on July 23rd, 1867. When she began teaching at Plains School around 1900, she lived with Miss Mary Detlor, the town librarian, in a house at 2059 Gore Street (now a Royal LePage Real Estate office). She walked daily to and from school, although in stormy weather, Arthur Lindley, who was secretary-treasurer of the school board, often drove her with his horse and buggy, or the cutter in winter. Edna Robinson recalled that when Miss Pattinson was walking home from school, she often stopped to talk politics with Edna's father, M.M. Robinson. These were often heated discussions, because Miss Pattinson was an ardent Liberal, while Bobbie Robinson was a Conservative. When prime minister Sir Wilfrid Laurier died, Miss Pattinson wore a black arm band.

Later, she travelled to and from Milton daily on the bus. Miss Pattinson taught for 50 years, most of them spent at "her" school on Plains Road. She was a very special person who influenced her pupils in many beneficial ways. Every Friday afternoon, there was a spelling bee for the senior students, while the younger ones listened. After school, several pupils were chosen to remain to wash the blackboards and help Annie Smale who was the caretaker at the school. Arthur Lindley received $25 a year for his work as secretary-treasurer of the school board. Each year, on the day before the Christmas concert, he would go to Stevenson's fruit market in Hamilton and spend the $25 on oranges and candies for the children. The mothers would fill Christmas stockings with these goodies, which Santa Claus distributed at the close of the concert.

Helen Pattinson's successor, Annette Marshall, who as Miss Huffman taught at the school for eight years, described Miss Pattinson as a "Jenny Wren" because she was small, quick, busy and always happy.

Because many of her pupils were interested in sports, Miss Pattinson encouraged team games such as baseball and football. At Christmas, there were always lavish programs of carols and plays, with parents and friends packing the hall.

When Helen Pattinson retired in 1934, the teachers of Halton County, the inspectors and many other well-wishers gathered at the Estaminet to pay tribute to this fine woman who had done so much for Burlington's children. She is buried in Union Cemetery, near her school. Her gravestone says "Teacher. [the name she was known by with affection] Helen Pattinson. 1867 to 1954."

HUFFMAN, Annette

When Helen Pattinson retired, she was replaced by a young Burlington native, Annette Huffman. To the new teacher, the task seemed tremendous. For one thing, there were 60 pupils at Plains School. The Senior IV class (Grade 8) consisted of 9 huge boys and 1 huge girl, a rather intimidating sight for the young teacher who was a very small person. Fortunately, the classroom had a platform across the front so that the new teacher could look down at her seated pupils! Furthermore, Miss Huffman was filling the place of a respected, experienced teacher.

Nevertheless, her years at the school were memorable. Miss Huffman continued her predecessor's encouragement of sports. One of the most exciting sports highlights was the day when Plains School played a challenge game with Burlington Central School. It was an away-from-home game for Miss Huffman's students, and although they lost by a narrow margin, they found the competition stimulating. Later, the School

Board put up an ice rink at the school. Students maintained the rink, and hockey and skating were enjoyed every day in winter.

The Christmas programs continued, too. Students loved the day when they were asked to climb the stairs to the attic to bring down the costumes. This was always accompanied by a further climb to the roof verandah to broaden the children's horizons with a view of the surrounding countryside!

In 1938, the Hamilton Normal School asked permission to use the school as a training school. Every week, six students arrived to observe the school programs in action and do practice teaching.

Miss Huffman always felt that her relationship with the inspectors was the best possible. On one occasion, J.M. Denyes, the inspector arrived at the school. He confided to Miss Huffman that his mind was not on his work that day. He had been listening on his car radio to reports coming from the site of a mine disaster in which several miners were entombed. After a quick consultation, it was decided to have the older students adjourn to the inspector's car. Almost 40 students crammed into the car, sat on the hood or stood on the running boards to listen to the radio coverage of the disaster, and experience a living lesson in current events.

Upon retirement, Miss Pattinson had given her successor much good advice on running the school. She added another piece of advice: "Get married". In 1942, Annette Huffman followed that advice, and retired from teaching. Her memories of the school were always happy ones.

The school was demolished to make way for highway expansion.

WOOD, Clarence

Some of the schools in the area served their communities for a century or more. However, Glenwood School at the corner of Glenwood School Drive and Guelph Line had a very short life span — just 26 years. The school was built on property which had belonged to Clarence Wood. The 200 acre Wood farm had originally extended to Drury Lane on the western extremity, and to New Street to the south. By the 1940s, most of it had been sold off for the construction of homes.

The Queensway Survey was built at the close of World War II to provide housing for servicemen under the Veterans' Land Act. With so many new families moving into the area, a new school was required to replace the overcrowded two-roomed Fisher's Corners School.

When Glenwood School opened on September 1st, 1947, it was considered to be one of the most up-to-date elementary schools in the province. Designed after an American style school, the eight classrooms included manual training and home economics rooms. There was also an auditorium, office, washrooms and storerooms, all built on a large concrete slab over which brown mastic tiles were laid. In 1950, four additional classrooms were built, and in 1953, a double kindergarten was added. This meant that there was an enrollment capacity of 450 in a one level school.

The school faced the northeast to eliminate the glare of the sun on the blackboards. Each classroom had its own exit door directly to the outside for fire safety. Very large windows reached to within three feet of the floor, giving the pupils an excellent view of the traffic on Guelph Line. This often proved to be a distraction for daydreamers!

For ventilation, there was a set of small windows above the blackboards, facing southwest. Because of the shortage of plaster in the post war years, the interior walls were covered with plywood. This modern school was opened officially by the Honourable Dana Porter, Minister of Education in the Tory government of the day.

To create a Glenwood School community, principal R.M.M. Acheson implemented home visits. Teachers visited pupils' homes, and parents visited the school on a regular basis. In time, teachers visited the homes of almost all of their pupils. This meant that teachers had to travel as far east as Appleby Line, north to Highway 5, south to Roseland, and west in the Queensway survey.

The Home and School organization was very active. Nearly 200 parents attended a meeting to resolve the controversial matter of milk delivery to the school. The issue was

Exterior of Glenwood School, Nelson Township, Ont. Note door to each classroom and wide windows, gently sloping roof, attractive entrance, playground space.

Opened Sept. 1947
Demolished 1978

Classroom in Glenwood School, showing clerestory windows, above the blackboard. Lampshades are made from plaskon moulding powder for better light. Photos Morton & Evans, Architects.

Glenwood School.

M.M. Robinson in uniform of British Empire Games, 1930.
—*Courtesy Edna Robinson*

resolved when it was decided to give Lakeshore Dairy a contract for one year, and Sani-Dairy the contract for the following year.

In 1973, this excellent school was closed because enrollment had fallen to 125 pupils. It is ironic that the school that was on the leading edge of school construction in 1947 became part of Burlington history so quickly. By 1978, the Halton Public School Board arranged for the school's demolition, and sold this valuable site to a developer. In 1992, the site is still a wasteland beset with legal and economic problems.

ROBINSON, M.M.

Have you ever wondered what M.M. Robinson did to have a secondary school named in his honour? It's a very interesting story.

Melville Marks Robinson was a native of Peterborough. Almost everyone knew him as M.M. or Bobby. While playing basketball in Hamilton, his teammates called him Robbie Robinson, which later became Bobby. He wore many different hats around Burlington.

He left school at 13 and took a job at the *Toronto News* as an office boy in the circulation department. Later, he became assistant sports editor at $8.50 a week. In 1910, he was hired as sports editor at the *Hamilton Spectator* at $15 a week, and later became city editor of that newspaper. One day in 1927, he was chatting with Howard Crocker who had been director of Athletics at the University of Western Ontario. They were deploring the fact that Canadian runners lacked the competition they needed to develop into top athletes in their fields. Crocker mentioned the Empire Festival which had been held in England in 1911. Bobby Robinson took up the idea immediately. He began lobbying for the establishment of the British Empire Games, which he wanted held in Hamilton. In 1928, he went to Amsterdam as manager of the Canadian Olympic Track and Field Team, and took the opportunity of selling the idea of the Empire Games abroad.

In order to develop the necessary facilities for such games, Hamilton had to have a stadium and an indoor swimming pool. T.B. McQuesten, then chairman of the Hamilton

Parks Board, convinced the city council that it would be worthwhile to spend the money needed. As a result, Civic Stadium and the Municipal Pool were built at a cost of $160,000.

Meanwhile, Bobby Robinson went abroad to approach other countries in the Empire. They were all enthusiastic, except for one. When Robinson met with Lord Derby in England, Derby insisted that the games weren't practical due to the Depression and lack of funds. Robinson told him that "If Britain won't play with us, we will have to turn south — to the United States." That convinced Lord Derby that Britain should compete! The British Empire Games were held in Hamilton in 1930, and are still being held, although now they are called the Commonwealth Games. The founder of the Games continued to manage Canadian Olympic and B.E.G. track teams until 1938.

In 1920, Bobby Robinson bought a 23 acre Maple Avenue farm, and became immersed in the wonders of agriculture. At first he grew raspberries, strawberries and other fruits, but later he turned exclusively to vegetables. His farm manager was Alex Barnes, a Mohawk Indian who, with his family, lived on the Robinson farm.

As with his other interests, Bobby Robinson threw himself into farming wholeheartedly. He became secretary-treasurer of the Ontario Fruit and Vegetable Growers Association from 1946 to 1959, secretary of the first Ontario Food Council from 1940 to 1957, and president of the Canadian Horticultural Council in 1957. The Ontario Food Terminal was established in Toronto largely due to his efforts, and he was a member of its board from 1946 to 1957. For 20 years, he was editor of the Ontario Fruit and Vegetable Growers Association's official publication, *The Grower*, influencing the industry extensively through his editorials and his column, "Speaking Frankly and with Logic." In recognition of his service to agriculture in Ontario, he was awarded an Award of Merit by the OFVGA in 1952, and received another from the Canadian Horticultural Council in 1972.

Having left school at an early age, Bobby Robinson knew the value of learning, and was a champion of education. For

M.M. Robinson with Minister of Education Wm. Davis at opening of M.M. Robinson School.   *—Courtesy Edna Robinson*

Kilbride School, 1953. Nancy Taylor Ramshaw, teacher.

many years, he served as chairman of the High School Board, and was involved in the development of education in the quickly expanding city. In 1959 when Aldershot, East Flamborough, Burlington and Nelson Township were amalgamated to form the city of Burlington, the Burlington Board of Education replaced the former Burlington High School Board, the Nelson Township Area Board, and part of the Flamborough Board. Bobby Robinson became the first chairman of the newly organized Board of Education.

Another of Bobby Robinson's concerns was health care in Burlington. In 1956, he and deputy reeve of Nelson Township, Eric Gudgeon, headed a citizens' committee which proposed that a modern hospital be built in the community. While almost everyone agreed that a hospital was needed, there was heated controversy over the location. One school of thought believed that it should be in the northern portion of Burlington, while another urged a central location. In the end, the hospital board purchased the present site from the federal and provincial governments for $24,578 for the construction of a 150-bed hospital.

In 1959, Bobby Robinson was named "Citizen To Be Remembered" for his contribution to education. When the new high school was opened on Upper Middle Road in September, 1963, it was appropriately named M.M. Robinson. Bobby Robinson died in 1974 at the age of 86, but he continued to receive honours. He was inducted into the Sports Hall of Fame in 1974, and into the Ontario Agricultural Museum's Hall of Fame in 1984.

Bobby Robinson's daughter, Edna, attended S.S. 14 at the head of Maple Avenue. Later, she was principal of Nelson High School, the first woman high school principal in Ontario. She also became a superintendent of education for the Halton Board of Education.

SMITH, Lawrie

Lawrie Smith, grandson of Burlington pioneer Hiram Smith, had developed 100 acres on the east side of Walker's Line, bought by his grandfather in 1854. Lawrie Smith's home is still standing near Walker's Line on Apple Valley Lane.

Colin Smith, Lawrie's brother, developed the 100 acre parcel called Ravenswood on the west side of Walker's Line. That had also been originally purchased by Hiram Smith.

Lawrie and Colin, as successful fruit growers, were exhibitors with the Royal Agricultural Winter Fair in Toronto from 1922 to the beginning of the Second World War, when the event was cancelled for the duration.

Much of the fine apple crop grown by Lawrie Smith, and later by Art Kemp, was exported overseas. The apples for export were carefully packed by hand in orchard boxes, although sometimes wholesalers from Toronto used lead-lined tea chests to transport apples in quantity. Apples for local use were packed in six-quart or bushel baskets. The orchards also produced pears, plums and sour cherries.

Before the formation of the first School Area Board in Burlington in 1942, each school section was under the jurisdiction of a 3 man school board. Each school section held an annual meeting of taxpayers, usually the fathers of the students of the local school. The purpose of this meeting, held on the first Wednesday after Christmas, was to elect the 3 trustees to the school section board.

Lawrie Smith and 2 other public-spirited gentlemen were responsible in 1913 for the organization of the Strathcona School Section. Later he represented Nelson township on the Burlington High School Board. When the first School Area Board was formed in 1942, Lawrie Smith became chairman, a position he held for two years. For another 8 years he carried on as a trustee.

He also found time to devote to the Nelson Township Council, serving for 4 years as a member. In addition, he was President of the Halton County Music Festival and an active supporter of the Home and School.

In recognition of the many years of service devoted to his community, Lawrie Smith School was named in his honour. Currently, this school is the site of the Burlington campus of Sheridan Community College.

MCNIVEN, James

In the middle of the 19th Century, the village of Kilbride was a very busy community. It had a large department store, a hotel, a wagon-maker's shop, a woollen mill, a tannery, a cooper's shop and a harness shop. Like Cumminsville, its neighbour a mile to the south, it had a population of 200. The first schoolhouse in this thriving area was in the home of the local magistrate, John Harris. There was also a log schoolhouse on the Coulson homestead, north of the village on No. 10 Sideroad.

In 1879, a fine new two storey school was built from local stone. It must have been a pleasant place for the children, for the schoolyard was bordered with lovely mature maple trees.

James McNiven was one of the trustees, and it was part of his job as secretary-treasurer to pay the teacher's salary every quarter. His son, Frank, attended Kilbride School from 1895 to 1903, in the days when the teacher's salary was $250 a year!

Over the years, the enrollment at Kilbride School dropped from 90 to 61. One of the schoolrooms was closed, causing a great deal of concern in the community. Later, enrollment increased so much that the unused classroom was re-opened, and a second teacher hired to share responsibilities.

In January, 1943, Nelson School Area No. 1 was formed, in keeping with the reorganization of administrative areas throughout Ontario. At this time, there was a tremendous controversy in the school area in the northern part of Nelson Township. Some parents wanted a graded school built in the area. Others thought it was a good idea, but wanted the new school built in Kilbride. Still others were adamant that the one-roomed schoolhouse provided the best type of education for their children. Finally, the eight-roomed Fairview School was built south of Lowville in 1954. It was the Board's intention to close all of the rural schools, but the opposition was so strong that Kilbride and Bell schools were left open. Parents had the choice of letting their children walk to the smaller schools, or be bussed to Fairview.

John McNiven was involved in this battle over education. He ran for the office of reeve of Nelson, warning taxpayers against the increase in taxes which the new school would mean for them. He was elected, but died early in 1950 without completing his term of office. His name is remembered in connection with McNiven Road in north Burlington.

But amalgamation had changed the pattern of development in the area. Before long, a new school was needed in the northern part of the newly formed city of Burlington. In 1959, the school board purchased three acres to the north of the old Kilbride school property, and made plans for a six-roomed school. The new school opened in September, 1961 with 190 pupils and a staff of eight, including six teachers. The principal was Florence Meares. The old stone school is now a residence.

Fairview School was closed in 1984 when an addition was put on Kilbride School. Students from Fairview were then transferred to Kilbride. The "new" Kilbride School now houses a branch of the Burlington Public Library which services the rural area of Burlington.

The Halton Region Conservation Authority bought the Fairview School building, and located its offices there.

LOCKHART, John

For 26 years, beginning in 1926, John A. Lockhart was the principal of Central Public School in Burlington. Like other principals of his era, he taught Grade 8. He was a strict disciplinarian, often feared by his pupils; yet, he brought out the best in each one. Each day began with oral arithmetic drill. Those who went through his Grade 8 class found the high school entrance exams quite easy.

Helen (Lindley) Langford recalls that one summer day, he came to her home to bring her a War Savings Certificate as a prize for excelling in the exams. During the war years, school children had the opportunity every week to purchase war savings stamps. They cost 25 cents each, and were pasted into a booklet with a total value of $4. It was a practical way for the children to contribute to the war effort and set aside money, too.

After completing his career in education, John Lockhart entered local politics, serving as mayor from 1957 to 1961.

One of the important accomplishments of his term of office was the establishment of an industrial and development committee with former mayor, Gordon Blair, as administrator. The purpose of the committee was to establish an environment which would attract industry. In 1958, Burlington had only 58 acres of fully serviced land available for industrial development. One of the first industries to come to the newly formed city was the Fuller Brush Company which moved from Hamilton. This move, the beginning of Burlington's industrial growth, hastened the demise of farming in the area.

DALGLEISH, Norman

For many years, children living in Aldershot attended a one-room schoolhouse on Howard Road. However, that was replaced by Maplehurst School on Plains Road East in 1911. Two years later, a second school was built on Plains Road West. This one was called Fairfield. This sturdy brick building had four rooms, only two of which were used until 1920. In the intervening years, the two upstairs rooms remained unfinished.

In 1935, Norman Dalgleish came to serve as principal at the school. During his years at Fairfield, the local population increased greatly, making it necessary for four more rooms to be added to the school. For a few years, this extra space was adequate, but after the Second World War, the baby boom plus the real estate boom boosted population and another four classrooms had to be added to Fairfield School again.

Norm Dalgleish was later principal of Glenview School which opened in the late 1950s when population mushroomed once again. After serving as principal of Lawrie Smith School for several years, he retired in 1971. Since then, he has been very active in the community. As a charter member of Aldershot Presbyterian Church, opened in 1955, he has been an avid fund-raiser. One of his favourite projects was monthly noon luncheons which he encouraged the staffs of Glenview, Fairfield and other nearby schools to attend. He is also remembered for his meat pie sales, another successful project of the Aldershot Women's Association.

Norman Dalgleish, Principal of Lawrie
Smith School, also of Glenview
1952-1962 and Fairfield, 1935-1952.
—*Courtesy Norman Dalgleish*

The official opening of Kilbride School, November 1960. Roy Coulter, chairman of
Board of Education, Florence Meares, principal, Rev. William Wilkinson, Kilbride
United Church, Stan Holton, M.P.P. Halton.   —*Courtesy Florence Meares*

His hobby, collecting farm tools, has proved to be useful to the community as well. Norm Dalgleish was very helpful in the identification and classification of the artifacts at the Ireland House in preparation for its opening as a museum.

When Fairfield School celebrated its 75th anniversary in 1988, Norman Dalgleish returned after an absence of 25 years to teach a history lesson to the students in "his" old school.

MEARES, Florence

From earliest times, Burlington parents always made sure that their children received the best education possible. In the 1830s, the youngsters of Port Nelson received their education at S.S. No. 2 Nelson, on Water Street (Lakeshore Road) near Walker's Line. By 1850, the school had 63 pupils, although the building was reported by the local superintendent to be "not in good repair."

When Port Nelson and Wellington Square amalgamated in 1873 as the village of Burlington, the school was abandoned, and a new one was built on Water Street between Guelph Line and Smith Avenue, just east of the present Lakeshore School. Called East End School, this building was torn down in 1919, and replaced by a four room red brick school which was constructed at a cost of $38,000. While the new school was being built, classes were held in the basement of Knox Presbyterian Church. By 1959, Burlington had expanded eastward so rapidly that the school was no longer in the east end of town. Therefore, the name was changed to Lakeshore School.

One of the first women principals to be employed by the Halton Board of Education was Florence Meares. She began her teaching career in the one-roomed Ash School (S.S. 17 Trafalgar) on Tremaine Rd. When Glenwood School opened in 1947, she served as vice-principal. In 1960, she became principal of Kilbride School. Four years later, when she became principal at Lakeshore School, it had expanded to 12 rooms with 450 students from Kindergarten to Grade 6, with two enrichment classes and a class for the hearing impaired. In just three years, enrollment grew to 950! To-day, there are about 125 students from Kindergarten to Grade 4 at that school.

S.S. #12, Limestone, 1942. Irma Rochefort (Coulson) teacher. First row – Glenna Coulson, Paul Coulson, Billy Shields, Gordon Harris. Second row – Roy Harris, Margaret Harris, Irma, Keith Coulson, Allan Baldwin.   —*Courtesy Irma Coulson*

S.S. #5, around 1912, Nelson Village School.   —*Courtesy Annie Smith James*

Miss Meares finished her outstanding career in education as principal at Elizabeth Gardens School.

During her retirement, she was a trustee for six years with the Halton Board of Education, as well as a volunteer in a great many non-profit charitable groups, organizations and boards. Because of this involvement, she was named Citizen of the Year for Burlington in 1987.

COULSON (Rochefort), Irma

In 1940, career opportunities for women were limited. A high school graduate could choose a career as a secretary, a nurse, a teacher, or a housewife. Irma Rochefort chose teaching as the only option she could afford.

When she graduated from Normal School in 1941, her first teaching assignment was at S.S. 12 Nelson, Limestone School on Derry Road. This was one of the more modern schools, having been built in 1933 to replace the original school which had burned in that same year. It boasted indoor washrooms and central heating. Most schools still had wood stoves, and were supplied by water from a neighbour's well, so Miss Rochefort felt herself very lucky. Her starting salary was $850 a year. She paid $25 a month for board.

Limestone School had one large room, so it was "open concept" long before that idea became popular in the 1970s. Manual Training and Home Economics were taught to Grade 7 and 8 students by itinerant teachers, so on some days, three teachers were sharing the classroom, all teaching different subjects!

The only audio-visual aids were the blackboards and boxes of chalk, as well as somebody's discarded piano and the teacher's own picture collection. The library consisted of a couple of shelves of books donated from the parents' home collections.

The course of studies was dictated by the Department of Education, and was recorded in the old "gray book". Irma was required to teach, among other things, the function of snow fences in rural areas. Since she had never seen one, and the students were well acquainted with their appearance, location and use, the students taught the teacher!

Religious education was mandated. Provincial regulations stated that "Every public and high school shall be opened with the Lord's Prayer and closed with reading of the Scriptures and the Lord's Prayer." Pupils at Limestone School also used to sing a closing hymn such as "Now The Day Is Over." Trustees could order the repeating of the Ten Commandments at least once a week, although to Irma Rochefort's knowledge, they never did. After talking about the Creation as described in the Bible, and having discussed God's work on each of the first six days, Mrs. Coulson recalls that a Grade 1 pupil said, "I know what He did next. He went back to work again and made babies!"

In those days, the teacher was also principal, social worker, baby sitter, secretary, consultant, co-ordinator and fount of all knowledge. Parents never questioned teaching methods or disciplinary actions, and there were no regular parent-teacher interviews. The teacher was responsible to the three man board of trustees who did the hiring and firing of the teacher and the caretaker. Mrs. Coulson recalls that one year when the inspector gave her a rather negative review, she tendered her resignation. The trustees refused to accept it, saying, "Don't pay any attention to him. We don't."

In 1943, the Nelson Township School Area was formed. The new board members were W.E. Breckon, Bradford Clements, Martin Lindley, Charles Readhead and W.L. Smith who was chairman. Marion Kerns was secretary for the new board, and as part of her duties was required to deliver supplies to the schools under the board's jurisdiction.

Since the amalgamation of Nelson with Burlington, and the building of graded schools in rural areas, one-roomed schools are no longer used as educational facilities. Limestone School is now a private residence owned by one of Irma Coulson's former students.

FISHER, Paul

Like so many of Burlington's other outstanding citizens, Paul Fisher played a varied part in the life of the community. As a descendant of Peter Fisher who built Shady Cottage on the farm where the Burlington Mall now stands, he was first and foremost a fruit grower. He graduated from the Ontario Agricultural College at Guelph in 1911, and farmed the original 200 acre grant, first with his father, then with his brother.

However, Paul Fisher was a well-known figure in town as well as on the farm. He loved to stroll down Brant Street in his kangaroo skin hat, and his Norfolk jacket, puffing on a corncob pipe. He knew everyone, and always enjoyed a friendly chat. As a gregarious person, it was inevitable that he should be involved in many local groups. He was a charter member of the Rotary Club of Burlington, and was its first president. He was chairman of the Inter-Urban Water Board of Burlington and Nelson, a member of the High School Board, and Clerk of Sessions for a local United Church of Canada congregation. Boy Scouts and Girl Guides were invited to camp on a wooded area on his property.

Perhaps Paul Fisher is best remembered for his role as chairman of the board of governors of the Joseph Brant Memorial Hospital. A moving force in the process of having the hospital built, he turned the sod at the official ceremony held in May, 1959. Residents of Burlington had contributed more than $300,000 toward the hospital in a massive fund-raising drive. Total cost of the facility, which opened its doors in January, 1961, was $3.7 million.

Paul Fisher's sudden death in the middle of a curling match in 1974 came as a shock to all who knew him. He was buried with other members of the Fisher family in the Pioneer Union Cemetery on Plains Road.

LUCAS, Ted

When Ted Lucas came to Burlington to serve as manager of the Royal Bank of Canada in 1938, his bank was the only one in town. The bank, at the corner of Brant and Water Streets (now Lakeshore Road) was originally one of the 126 branches of the Traders Bank. It was built on what had previously been the site of the Galloway and Baxter store. The official opening was on August 8th, 1900. Office hours were 10 a.m. to 3 p.m. on weekdays, and on Saturdays from 10 a.m. to 1 p.m. The bank was also open from 7 to 9 on Saturday evening, for the convenience of farmers.

Traders Bank was absorbed by the Royal Bank of Canada in 1912. The original building was torn down to make way for the present one. Until 1945, it was still the only bank in town. Even after other branches and other banks were established in Burlington, this solid building remained as the main branch for the Royal Bank. It is still a branch, although the main office is now on Harvester Road.

Ted Lucas and his family lived in an apartment over the bank, as at that time it was the custom for managers to live on the premises. He was the longest-serving manager the branch ever had, holding his position from 1938 until 1962.

DETLOR, Mary

One of the most important institutions in any community is the library. From 1908 until 1935, Mary Detlor was the librarian in Burlington. She not only performed the usual duties of such a person, but also served as book vendor, caretaker and general maintenance person.

Burlington's library had its start in 1872 when the village council decided to vote $56 for the purchase of books from the Toronto Board of Education. The collection was kept in the hallway at S.S. No. 1 Nelson — Central School. There was an annual fee of 50 cents, and the library was open from 2 p.m. to 5 p.m. on Saturday afternoons. A borrower could be prosecuted for failing to check out a book with the librarian!

As the years went by, the village council could see the advantages of this service, and other small sums of money were provided to purchase books. In 1883, there were 1,112 books in the collection, and the annual circulation was 2,200. The following year, it was decided to move the collection to the home of Henry Berry on Brant Street.

In 1906, one of Burlington's prominent citizens who had earlier moved to Toronto, John Waldie, offered the village $1,000 to build a library, provided that a suitable site was located. The library board chose a lot on the west side of Brant Street, at the site of the present City Hall. Since the municipal offices on Elizabeth Street were bulging at the seams, it was agreed to provide office space for the village clerk in the new library building.

It was to these premises that Mary Detlor came to take up her duties. O.T. Springer, the village clerk, assisted her by combining his regular duties with those of part-time librarian so that the library could stay open longer hours. Even then, the service was not what we are used to to-day. Borrowers were shown a list of books from which to choose, and the books were removed from the shelves by the librarian.

In 1918, the library had 182 members. There were 4,410 books to choose from, in addition to several magazines — Macleans, Reader's Digest, Canadian Ladies Journal, Life, Current History, and Good Housekeeping. Circulation that year was over 4,000.

Early in 1935, Mary Detlor suffered a heart attack while sitting at her desk in the library. She died in April of that year after serving as librarian for 27 years.

ANGUS, Dorothy

After Mary Detlor's death, Mae Holtby took over as librarian for a short time while a permanent replacement was found. The library board's choice was Dorothy Angus, a young widow. She was the right choice, for over the next 27 years (the magic number for Burlington librarians, apparently!) she made a tremendous contribution to the library. She introduced arts and craft shows, musical evenings, flower shows and story hours for the children. In 1936, she dressed up as a stork at Canada's first national book fair in Toronto, and won a $50 prize which she used to buy books for the library.

War brides who arrived in Burlington besieged the library with requests for information on Canadian housekeeping. Dorothy Angus made a special effort to help these young women adjust to their new way of life. On one occasion, Mrs. Angus discovered that a member of the library board had taken time, while in the library, to help a war bride plan a simple dinner menu. Mrs. Angus discussed this with the board member, and it was decided that she should arrange for a series of lectures, given by a teacher from MacDonald Institute at the Ontario Agricultural College (now the University of Guelph) to help the newcomers to plan, buy for and cook Canadian meals.

First library building shared with Municipal Offices, Brant St., around 1945.
—Courtesy Hamilton Public Library

During her years at the library, Dorothy Angus also began having small exhibitions of paintings by local artists, thus giving a boost to Burlington talent. Another of her popular innovations was a series of puppet shows which the children loved.

A native of Dundas, Dorothy Philp came to Burlington as a bride when she married Arthur J. Angus. She was widowed in 1924. Always active in the community, she was the first secretary of the Burlington Horticultural Society, a member of the I.O.D.E. and the Order of the Eastern Star, and the first woman elder of Wellington Square United Church. Later, she was a member of the Ontario, Canadian and American Library Associations.

There is an interesting story about Dorothy Angus and a tramp. During the Depression, many unemployed men went "on the road" because they were unable to find work. Dorothy Angus had pear trees in her garden. One day, when a tramp came to her door asking for food, she told him he could have some pears if he would pick them. He did so, filling his pockets, then came to the window to thank her. At the time, Dorothy was frying eggplant, and when the tramp remarked that it smelled so good, she gave him a plateful. Later, she saw him taking the pears from his pocket and putting them back by the tree. Since she had given him a hot meal, he didn't feel entitled to the pears, and was leaving them for someone else. Dorothy Angus once asked the police chief why so many tramps came to her door, and he told her that her address was written on the wall of the jail cell as a good place to get a meal in Burlington!

When she became librarian, Mrs. Angus immediately began to brighten the library's quarters on Brant Street. As both the library and the municipal offices continued to expand, it was agreed that the library needed its own building. In 1952, Dr. A.H. Speers' home on Elizabeth Street was bought for this purpose, and was renovated at a cost of $35,000. At this time, the library was open eight hours a week, and Mrs. Angus was paid $400 a year. Nevertheless, she worked hard to keep the library growing. The first branch was opened in 1960 in the basement of the Dominion Store at Zellers Plaza in Aldershot. Other branches were later opened at Skyway Plaza and at Kilbride.

The library itself underwent changes. In 1956, the building at 482 Elizabeth street was expanded to make room for an art gallery, and a garage for a bookmobile. In 1957, at a Civic Night held at the Lido Deck of the Brant Inn, Dorothy Angus was honoured as Burlington's "Citizen To Be Remembered", an award sponsored by the Optimist Club.

After her retirement in 1962, Dorothy Angus lived for many years on Ontario Street before moving into Maple Villa Nursing Home. She did not live to see the establishment of the present Central Library in 1970. The library has come a long way since its humble beginnings. In 1990, the annual budget was $4.5 million. There are now over 400,000 publications in the collection, with a staff of 107 handling a circulation of 1.2 million.

REDDY, Ida

When Burlington's population quadrupled in 1958, with the amalgamation of Nelson Township and East Flamborough, demand for library services quickly outgrew availability. Dr. Speers' house which was being used for the library had had two additions, and was still overflowing.

In January, 1961, Ida Reddy was hired as deputy librarian, and when Mrs. Angus retired the following year, she was appointed chief librarian. Miss Reddy was well qualified for the job, having been chief librarian at a branch of the Toronto Public Library. She was a very people-oriented librarian who spent a lot of time with the patrons and members of the library board. Under her direction, the library became less formal, with the staff encouraged to provide patrons with superior service. In 1962, the art gallery area of the library was transformed into the children's room where special programs could be held, and the garage was converted to a storage space.

Ida Reddy worked closely with Frank Rose, chairman of the library board, who made presentations to the city council for money for a new library building. As a public relations man, Frank Rose insisted that presentations, written by Ida

Burlington Public Library, Elizabeth St., 1952-1970.

Lucille Galloway and Wendy Schick.
—Courtesy Burlington Public Library

Reddy and edited by himself, be short, snappy and well rehearsed. The result was worth the effort.

However, Ida Reddy did not remain at the Burlington Public Library long enough to work in the new library. In 1968, she accepted a position as assistant to the director of the South Central Regional Library System based in Hamilton.

GALLOWAY, Lucille

In 1968, Lucille Galloway was lured away from the position as head of the technical services department at the Hamilton Public Library to become chief librarian at Burlington. Shortly after this, Council voted $500,000 for the construction of the present building on New Street.

With the completion of the new building imminent, Miss Galloway began stockpiling books to fill the shelves, and hired three professional librarians to provide up-to-date library services for the community. The building opened in November, 1970, and was enlarged five years later as demand for services continued to grow.

When Mrs. Galloway retired in 1985, Burlington Public Library was immersed in modern technology including computerized library catalogues and book check-out, videotapes, audio-cassettes and visual compact discs with ROM (Read Only Memory).

Those who visit the public library on New Street will have noticed the town bell on the property. This bell was purchased by the town council in 1894, and was installed in a bell tower on the town hall on Elizabeth Street. The bell was rung daily at 7 a.m., noon, 1 p.m. and 6 p.m., as well as for fires and other emergencies. The bell was removed in the 1950s, and put into storage. At one time, it was stolen, but quickly recovered when a policeman noticed a car that seemed to be riding exceptionally low to the road. There is also a story that in the 1960s, William Gilbert, then chairman of the library board, saw a man with a pickup truck take the bell from behind the works department building, saying that it was to be used for scrap metal. Mr. Gilbert retrieved the bell and established a fund so that the bell could be installed in its present location beside the library.

ANDERSON, Joseph

Before 1892, the streets of Burlington were lighted only by the moon and the light radiating from homes and businesses. In that year, however, coal oil lamps were ordered from a Montreal firm, and installed at the cost of $1.50 each. Joseph Anderson was designated as the first official lamp lighter, a position he held until 1897.

We hear of Mr. Anderson again in 1900 when his name came up at the first council meeting of that year. At that meeting, it was moved that he be appointed road commissioner, constable, truant officer, chief of the fire brigade, lamp lighter and caretaker of the town hall at a total salary of $365 per year. When the vote was taken, the motion was not carried. Councillor Ogg then amended the motion to read that J.W. Henderson be appointed constable at $55 a year, and William Armstrong take the rest of the jobs at $300. This amendment was lost, too.

Next it was moved that Thomas Sneath be appointed to light lamps "in the west end, same as last year at $44." This was carried. There were still five positions to fill. Two more names were put forward, and these motions were lost as well. By this time, the clerk must have been frantic!

It was finally agreed, in a three to two vote, that Joseph Anderson become road commissioner, constable, caretaker of the town hall, truant officer, chief of the fire brigade and lamp lighter in the east end at $360 a year.

After all that, by May 2nd of that same year, Joseph Anderson tendered his resignation from all of those positions. Perhaps he had just bitten off more than he could chew.

SMITH, Lee J.

When Burlington became a town in 1914, it was a quiet little place. One constable was quite enough to handle the occasional case of rowdyism, reckless driving or allowing a dog to run at large. Constables came and went. In 1911, four were hired and fired within a few months.

In 1916, however, the town appointed Lee J. Smith as constable. This was an association that lasted until his retirement in 1956. Lee Smith soon became Chief of Police, and under his guidance the department grew and developed into a modern police force. Improvements began almost immediately, for the same year that he was hired, a telephone was installed in the police office, and his salary was raised to $17.80 a week.

At this time, the Burlington police handled an average of less than one offender a week! To provide Chief Smith with some time off, in 1917 Bert Dunham was appointed special constable. He worked every other Sunday for $2. There was also one night constable, Allan Mitchell Sr.

As automobiles proliferated, traffic violations did, too. Over the years, Chief Smith's staff grew to four full-time officers. In 1947, the department received its first car, a Ford. Headquarters were in the town hall on Elizabeth Street where there were four cells beneath the office. By this time, the department was handling between 400 and 500 cases a year.

When Chief Smith retired after 40 years' service to the town, he was well respected for the professionalism he brought to law enforcement in Burlington.

SMITH, A.R.

The First World War had just ended when A.R. Smith moved his family from Hamilton to Burlington. He had been a worker in a munitions factory, but in 1918 had the opportunity to join the police force in Burlington. He was to patrol Highway 2 between the Hamilton and Toronto borders as a motorcycle officer. When the Ontario Provincial Police was formed, he continued his motorcycle patrols.

The Smith family moved into a house on Martha Street at the corner of Maria. The horse and wagon bearing their household goods bogged down in the mud on Brant Street before reaching their new home.

Annie Smith, A.R.'s daughter, was five years old when she started kindergarten at Central School. She remembers proudly setting out in a blue dress with a big hair bow, and carrying a school bag with a slate, slate pencil and a rag with which to clean the slate.

Across from the Smith's house on Maria Street was the radial car barn and a vacant lot. The radial cars ran between

Hamilton and Oakville, and were constantly coming and going. The children loved to play baseball in the field which is now Lion's Club Park. Often, they roller skated up Brant Street all the way to Highway 5 without seeing a car.

There were many skating parties at the arena on Elgin Street. The building had a change room with a huge wood stove, just the place to warm up on a cold winter night. Sometimes the young people walked to Brant's Pond to skate, or even to the golf course to toboggan on the hills. In those halcyon days, the young people were never afraid to walk anywhere in town, even after dark. Few had the luxury of automobiles, and so they walked everywhere.

Annie Smith enjoyed her years at high school, and felt that the principal, James MacFarlane Bates, made every subject interesting. She especially enjoyed botany and zoology, and this eventually led her into a career in nursing. During the Second World War, she worked with Dr. Speers, the medical health officer, and taught first aid and home nursing at the high school and the town hall.

HUNT, Harvey

Just before the Second World War, Nelson council decided that the township should have its own police protection, rather than pay Chief Lee Smith of Burlington $400 a month to provide this service. The decision was reached after a great deal of discussion, for some council members favoured the use of Chief Smith's services, while others believed that the provincial police should take over the area.

As a result of the council's decision, Harvey Hunt was appointed chief constable for Nelson Township. Hunt had no experience in police work, but he was a well-built man, standing six feet two inches, and weighing over 200 pounds. Besides, he was a lifelong resident of Nelson Township, and was well-known and respected throughout the community. He farmed on Highway 5, between Guelph Line and Walker's Line, on the farm he had inherited from his father. Edward Hunt had come from Bromley, Kent in England as a Barnardo boy, and, after working on various farms, had eventually purchased this property.

A.R. Smith, Ethel & Annie in 1917.
—*Courtesy Annie Smith James*

Harvey Hunt of the O.P.P. at his farm, now the
site of Tansley United Church.
—*Courtesy Shirley Bottaro, Grimsby*

Harvey Hunt's duties were varied. In addition to other policing responsibilities, he served as truant officer, weed inspector, welfare officer and water inspector. He could be reached any time by phoning 16 ring 14. If he was out in the field, his wife would fetch him immediately. He would be in uniform and on duty within minutes. Sometimes he was called out to warn youngsters about eating grapes from farmers' vines. On several occasions, he was summoned by lakeshore residents to chase away illegal fishermen. In these cases, he did not respond too quickly, always giving the fishermen time to catch enough for their supper.

The Hunt family was accustomed to having strangers at the table for meals. Often, Chief Hunt would bring prisoners home for lunch, on their way to the lock-up in Milton. He and Chief Lee Smith annually collected food for hampers for the needy at Christmas, and always spent Christmas Eve and part of Christmas Day delivering them. In 1955, this evolved into the Christmas Welfare Committee, and later became the Christmas Bureau.

After amalgamation in 1958, Harvey Hunt transferred to the Burlington City Police Department where he served as inspector of personnel until his retirement in 1962.

Harvey Hunt's brother, Fred, was postmaster at Freeman and had the store which was later purchased by the Pridmores.

BELL, Harris

In 1923, Harris Bell's father was approached by a representative of Nelson Township to provide a team of horses for use in road work. Mr. Bell had the horses, but said that there was no one to drive them. The township man looked at Harris and asked, "What about him?" So it was that 16 year old Harris Bell began a 49 year career in road work.

Most roads were still mud, built to accommodate horse and buggy traffic. They were levelled or widened with a wooden-wheeled grader drawn by three teams of horses. Harris earned $6 a day on the job.

Where stone was used, it came by boxcar from Dundas to the Freeman or Maple Avenue stations where it was transferred to horsedrawn wagons. The gravel would be dumped

Rock cutting on Dundas St.

—*Courtesy Irma Coulson*

Town Hall and the Fire Hall. Firemen at Fire Hall, Elizabeth St., around 1950.

—*Courtesy Frank Armstrong, Photographer Arnold Wilbur*

New Fisher's Corners School (S.S. #14 Nelson) on the southeast corner of Guelph Line & Queen Elizabeth Way, was closed in 1947. It was used as St. Christopher's Mission Church until 1954.
—Courtesy Florence Meares

ost Office, Brant St., next to Municipal Offices.
—Courtesy Dorothy Turcotte

Brant Inn fire, 1925.

Brant Inn fire, 1925.

Brant Inn fire, 1925.

—*Courtesy Anne Smith James*

Road gang on Locust St., around 1915.

—*Courtesy Ivan Cleaver*

on the roads, then levelled with the grader. It would then be sprinkled with water and rolled. Brant Street, Maple Avenue, Guelph Line and Cedar Springs Road were all serviced in this way. Teams were provided by the Powell and Robertson families of Nelson Township. In time, Nelson put in its own quarry to supply gravel.

There was one snow plough for Nelson, and one for Burlington. In 1930, the township bought a tractor and leaning wheel grader. In 1941, its fleet also consisted of a motorized grader which Harris Bell operated. After one severe storm, it was found that the Burlington plough could not do an adequate job, so Harris was called upon to use the township's plough on Burlington streets.

Harris Bell succeeded John Breckon as road superintendent when John died suddenly in 1944. His responsibilities included hiring and firing employees, keeping track of work time and the financial books, and reporting regularly to the Department of Highways and the township council.

VIII

POLITICS

Much of the story of Burlington's development from a rural village into a fine 20th century city can be told through the achievements of the men and women who had the drive and ambition to enter politics. Those who chose to become involved at the municipal level played as important a part in shaping the city as those at the provincial and federal levels. Mistakes were made, arguments took place, but great strides were taken in moving Burlington from village to small town, and finally to the city it is to-day.

ALLEN, James

When the villages of Port Nelson and Wellington Square joined in 1873 to become the village of Burlington, James Allen was one of the councillors elected to serve under Reeve John Waldie. Allen was well-known in town as the owner of the carriage works at the corner of Brant and Maria Streets. He was born in 1835, and at the age of 25, married Clementina McLaren. They raised a family of five daughters, four of whom married into well-known local families. The Allens lived in the house now known as Pilkey House, at the corner of Elizabeth and Maria Streets. This house was on land where an early Kerns house had stood.

James Allen was the village's first clerk-treasurer, and served in this capacity for many years. In 1897, his salary was $200, with $10 extra being paid for registering births, deaths and marriages. In 1900, his basic salary was the same, but he received $10.60 for registrations. He also was paid $8 to cover election expenses.

James' brother, George, for many years had a successful tinsmith and hardware business at the corner of Brant and Pine Streets. He served on the town council, and was reeve from 1906 to 1908. Another brother, John, was in partnership with George for a time, but later moved to Waterdown.

A fourth brother in this family was Joseph. His son, James S. Allen, was also active in the community. When electricity came to town in 1900, his tinware business manufactured the shades for the first electric lights available for private homeowners. Meanwhile, the village clerk was selling off the coal oil street lamps and poles for $1 each!

James S. Allen later became mayor of Burlington from 1925 to 1928. This member of the Allen family met a sad end. One morning, after picking up his mail at the post office, and stopping to chat with an employee of Virtue Motors, he went for his regular morning walk along the steep embankment at the waterfront. Shortly after, two teenaged boys noticed a body in the water. They rushed for help, and the body was pulled up onto the grass. It was ex-mayor Allen. At an inquest, the verdict was death by drowning. Evidence showed that Mr. Allen, age 76, had suffered a dizzy spell, been stunned in the fall down the embankment, and fallen face down into the water.

PETTIT, Mary S.

Back in the 1940s, politics was still a man's game. That didn't prevent Mary Pettit from giving it a try. Born in Hornby in 1888, she began her life as Mary Robertson. In 1913, she graduated from the nursing school at Guelph General Hospital, and, soon after, married Harry Pettit.

While raising her sons, Murray and William, she took an active part in the community. For many years, the family lived at Freeman on the 200 acre family farm on the south side of what is now the Queen Elizabeth Way between Guelph Line and Walker's Line. The house was called Prospect Lodge, and in 1937 the Pettits turned it into a successful tourist home.

In addition to all of this, Harry Pettit was Halton County clerk and treasurer. When he died in 1937, the farm was divided into five acre lots and sold, but Mary continued to operate Prospect Lodge.

Mary got her first taste of politics in 1936 when she was chairman of the Nelson Township Welfare Board. Her political career began in earnest in 1939 when she made the headlines as the first woman to be elected to municipal office in Nelson Township. She served as councillor until 1945, when she was elected deputy reeve, the first woman deputy reeve in Nelson. The following year, she was elected reeve of Nelson Township.

Mary Pettit was very conscientious in dealing with her responsibilities. It is said that during one heavy snowfall, she followed the snow plough in her car to make sure that it opened up "the proper places". Although a liberated woman in many ways, she still made tea for the councillors at the end of their meetings.

In 1949, Mary Pettit achieved another "first" when she was named Halton County warden, a position that required her to preside at all county council meetings. At the same time, she was chairman of the county board of health. Health and social welfare were always her chief concerns during her political career. In 1945, she ran as Liberal candidate for the riding of Halton during a provincial election but was defeated.

After moving to Milton in the mid 1950s, she immediately became involved in politics again, being elected to council in 1956 and as deputy reeve in 1958. In 1960, she was elected reeve, and would almost certainly have been re-elected for a second term if she had not died suddenly of a heart attack. She is buried in Greenwood Cemetery in Burlington, and remembered by many for her devoted efforts on behalf of the Halton County Public Health Unit and Halton Centennial Manor.

SMITH, Maxwell

One of the most outstanding and ingenious municipal politicians in Burlington's history was M.C. (Max) Smith. He was reeve of Burlington from 1908 to 1915. Then, when the village became a town, he was the first mayor, serving in that office from 1915 to 1916, and again in 1919.

Nowadays, politicians have to mind their "p's and q's", but they were not always under such close public scrutiny. When a new waterworks system was proposed in 1909, the

SUPPORT
MARY S. PETTIT

PROVINCIAL LIBERAL
CANDIDATE

**RESPONSIBILITIES GRAVITATE TO THOSE
WHO CAN SHOULDER THEM**

VOTING DAY, MONDAY, JUNE 4

Printed at the office of The Gazette Printing Co., Burlington

Flyer asking for support for Mary S. Pettit.

M.C. Smith.
—*Courtesy Joseph Brant Museum*

estimated cost was $50,000. Many residents thought this was a lot of money to add to the tax bill. Consequently, the matter was put to a public vote. Those in opposition went to the trouble of going to the registry office in Milton and making a list of those who they knew were in favour of the waterworks but were not eligible to vote because they were not property owners. This list was given to the returning officer so that he would know who to turn away from the polls.

When Reeve Smith heard about the list, he staged a diversion so that the list could be slipped away from the returning officer. On election day, Bill Brush, owner of the Queen's Hotel (now Sherwood Inn) drove one of his fast horses past the polling place on Brant Street, cracking the whip and making as much noise as possible. Of course everyone indoors rushed to the windows to see what was going on, and when it was all over, the infamous list had mysteriously disappeared. When the ballots were counted, the new waterworks had passed by a margin of 42 votes.

About the same time, Max Smith was involved in another coup for Burlington. Erosion on the waterfront had always been a problem. By 1908, it was so severe that David Henderson, the Member of Parliament for Halton asked the government to build a breakwater at Burlington. Although the bank was in danger of sliding into the lake, nothing happened.

Reeve Smith petitioned the government himself, but still nothing happened. Finally, he had a complete set of plans for a revetment wall drawn up by an engineer. He took them to Ottawa himself, and presented them to the recently appointed Minister of Public Works who was an acquaintance of Smith's. As it turned out, Smith also knew the minister's secretary, so he was greeted warmly.

The new secretary did not know that the federal government only became involved with improvements to harbours for ocean-going vessels. He suggested that Smith have the plans approved by the chief engineer. The engineer looked at the plans, clearly just sent down from the minister's office, and added his approval to what he assumed was the minister's. When Smith finally saw the minister, and told him that the plans had been approved by the chief engineer, the minister added his signature.

Thus it was that Burlington got its breakwater, the only one ever built at a fresh water harbour by federal money. Of course, this all finally came out in the Public Works office in Ottawa, but by that time the wall had been built.

That wall has long since been replaced by a new one at Spencer Smith Park. Originally, there was a narrow strip of parkland along the lakeshore, with a steep embankment covered with large stones. Between this and the breakwater was an expanse of water where local people and summer visitors anchored their boats. This has been filled in to create the present Spencer Smith Park.

Before he became involved in politics, Max Smith was well-known around town as a fruit grower and broker. He and his father, J.C. Smith, were partners in operating a fruit farm on Lakeshore Road. In 1909, a busy year for him, he founded the Niagara Brand Spray Company Limited which produced sulphur and other chemicals used by farmers. The business was located at Freeman, and continued to operate even after Smith sold his interest in it in the 1930s.

Always one step ahead of the world, Maxwell Smith owned the first car in Burlington. It was a single-cylinder Rambler, bought in 1902 and painted fire-engine red. There is another Max Smith legend that claims he was responsible for the white lines on our highways! It is said that when the Toronto to Hamilton highway was being paved in 1914, Smith and some others were watching the concrete being poured. There was some discussion about how cars could be prevented from running into each other when they went around the sweeping bend. "Paint a white line down the middle," Max Smith said. And they did. Perhaps Max Smith got this idea from his father, J.C. Smith who had painted the curb on Lakeshore Road at Rambo Creek so that vehicles would not go astray in the fog.

In 1906, Maxwell Smith purchased Chestnut Hall on Lakeshore Road for $6000. This house is now in front of the Brant's Landing condominium complex. Originally, it stood farther back on the property. This piece of land was owned by many outstanding Burlingtonians. Its first owner was Catherine Brant, Joseph's wife. Then it was owned by William and Augustus Bates who passed it down first to Augustus' daughter Rachel, then to William's son Philo, who was a lake boat captain. Up until this time, no known house was built on the property, but by 1872 Chestnut Hall had been built. When Amanda Baxter purchased it six years later, she made many changes to the existing building, and created a gracious Victorian mansion. When Max Smith bought the property, he added an interesting touch of his own in the form of an elaborate screened back porch.

When the house was moved to its present site and renovated, it was discovered that the building may be older than originally believed, and it may have been built by Philo Bates. During renovations, evidence of a cupola was found in the attic, and the basement had very old hardware and doors, indicating that it was an old house even when Amanda Baxter purchased it in 1878. The late Arthur Wallace, heritage architect, examined the house and reached these conclusions.

Maxwell Smith's children were Maxine, who married late in life, Dennis, and Peter. Dennis became a doctor and worked on ships to Bermuda. Later, he settled in Kirkland Lake. One Hallowe'en, he dressed in a grass skirt. As a prank, someone held a lighted cigarette lighter to the skirt, and Dennis burned to death. His bride gave birth to a daughter eight months later in Alberta where her parents lived.

MILLWARD, W.C.

From the time the W.C. Millwards moved to Smith's Lane (now Smith Avenue) in 1939, there was never a dull moment in their family life. Cec Millward was an electrician, working at that time at Firestone in Hamilton. When he left his job there he opened his own business, W. C. Millward and Son Electrical Contractors, in Burlington. During the building boom of the 1950s, the company wired hundreds of new homes in the area. His son George is still running the company.

Cec Millward grew up in Winona where his father was a well-known farmer and carpenter. In 1927, he married Norah Graves, and at first they had a farm in Vineland. For a while, they lived on the Beach Strip, then finally settled down at the Smith's Lane address. At that time, there were only four houses on the street.

In the 1940s, Cec became interested in politics. In the provincial election of 1946, he ran for the CCF (Co-operative Commonwealth Federation, the forerunner of the present NDP), competing against A.S. Nicholson for the Progressive Conservatives, and his friend Hughes Cleaver for the Liberals. Cleaver won. A lot of people were surprised that Cec ran for a socialist party, and some didn't associate with him after that. Nevertheless, he was well liked, and in 1947 became president of the Chamber of Commerce.

At about this time, he and three other men — Sam Ferguson, Harry Saunders and Frank Ellerbeck — got together to organize the Burlington Boys and Girls Band, which later evolved into the Burlington Teen Tour Band. Elgin Corlett was the first bandmaster.

Another of Cec Millward's accomplishments was the founding of the Parent Teacher Association at Lakeshore School. A man of many interests, Cec also loved hunting and fishing. At one time, he edited *Tight Lines*, newsletter of Rainbow Ranch, a private trout club at Campbellville, and he was one of the owners of the Cross Lake Hunting and Fishing Club in Haliburton. In fact, he was such an avid fisherman that when the family moved from the Beach Strip to Smith's Lane, he was scheduled to go on a fishing trip. He did go, leaving everything organized in advance to be handled by others!

Cec Millward died in November, 1991, at the age of 91.

FELLOWES, William

William Fellowes came to Canada from England in 1921 after serving in the First World War. Having been raised on a farm, he searched first for farm work, and was employed on a farm at Norval. After he married, he and his wife operated a two acre market garden north of Georgetown. His wife sold eggs and garden produce in Georgetown, while Bill Fellowes worked in the stone quarry at Glen Williams.

Herb Lindley, Harold Forrest, Wm. Fellowes at Lawn Bowling Club,
Shadeland Ave. & Plains Rd.

William Fellowes in the strawberry patch on
Shadeland Ave. —*Courtesy Mary Swan*

A two acre farm is not very large, so in 1929, the Fellowes bought 15 acres in Aldershot from George Filman. Their house was on Shadeland Avenue, now #903, just south of Townsend. The farm extended to the present Teal Avenue.

At the same time, Mr. Fellowes obtained water rights to a pond which George Filman had created by damming up the creek. He recalls that he used the pond for irrigation, and that later, the banks of the pond were attractively planted by a subsequent owner, Mrs. Smith. By 1954, the irrigation system covered the Fellowes' entire 15 acres.

Their first crop of the year was early cabbage in June, and the season ended with the celery and pear crops in November. The Fellowes' most profitable crop was Keiffer pears which were sold to a Grimsby canning factory in late fall for export to England.

The "Dirty Thirties" were difficult years. To supplement his income, Mr. Fellowes contracted with Flamborough Council to snowplough the cinder path which extended from Del Filman's Corner (now the intersection of King Road and North Shore Boulevard) to the Royal Botanical Gardens. The path was used by pupils attending Maplehurst and Fairfield Schools, so he had to start work at 5 a.m. in order to have the path cleared by 8. Using his own horse and plough, he was paid 50 cents an hour.

Bill Fellowes was also involved with the establishment of Aldershot Cold Storage which was started in the 1930s by R.L. Scott. Mr. Scott had to enlist 100 members at $100 each in order to get financial assistance from the provincial and federal governments. When Aldershot Cold Storage was later sold to Harry Wald, Mr. Fellowes was a member of the board of directors.

In 1938, Bill Fellowes was elected to East Flamborough council. At that time, council was responsible for providing Relief for the unemployed. At the first council meeting Mr. Fellowes attended, the Relief items on the agenda included:

    Red and White Store – Relief Acct. $13.00
    Bruce Sinclair General Store – Relief Acct. $40.82
    Canada Bread – Relief Acct. $1.04
    Lakeside Dairy – Relief Acct. $9.99

Later, Mr. Fellowes left council and was elected school trustee for Maplehurst School area, followed by an appointment to the Waterdown High School Board.

In 1954, Mr. Fellowes sold his property to J. Cooke for the Birdland Development, and granted him the right-of-way to extend Townsend Avenue east of Shadeland. After the sale of the farm, Mr. Fellowes continued to grow flowers in his greenhouse.

Having some free time at last, he joined the Aldershot Bowling Club which had been started in 1929. At that time, it was on the Godwin property next to the present XL gas bar on Plains Road East. In winter, the bowling green doubled as a community skating rink. When the Godwin property was sold, George Filman donated land for a new green on Shadeland Avenue. Members all pitched in to plough, level and plant the new green, and afterwards, to maintain it. The bowling green was closed in the 1960s when the City of Burlington opened new greens at the Seniors' Centre.

Mr. Fellowes also assisted in the organization of the Aldershot Senior Citizens' Group. At age 92, he continued to attend St. Matthew-on-the-Plains Anglican Church, being the oldest member of the congregation.

SMITH, E.W. (Ted)

Twenty-four years of service to the public is an achievement worthy of note! E.W. (Ted) Smith was councillor from 1936 to 1944, deputy reeve from 1945 to 1947, reeve from 1948 to 1950, mayor for six years, then councillor following that position.

When Burlington's new arena on New Street was proposed in the late 1940s, Mr. Smith was one of its champions. In 1950, he spoke in favour of a $40,000 debenture to raise the remaining funds needed for the project. The overall cost of the arena was expected to be $129,970, including $10,000 for the land, $97,470 for the contractor, and $22,500 for the refrigeration equipment. As a debenture would erase the project's deficit, it would be eligible for a $10,000 grant from the government.

Residents of Burlington had shown a keen interest in the building of the new arena. A few weeks before the opening, when word circulated that the artificial ice was being put in, curiosity drew citizens to the arena to watch. Many of these soon found themselves being recruited to help. At one time, there were 100 volunteers spreading, packing or levelling crushed ice between the miles of pipes on the floor of the arena. At the opening, Mayor Smith expressed appreciation for the help that had made it possible to hold the opening on schedule.

When the arena was officially opened in 1951, Mayor Smith dropped the puck for the face-off between the Burlington Mohawks Intermediate OHA team and the Nicholson Lumber Kings. A good crowd turned out to see the Mohawks win by a score of 12 to 3.

BLAIR, Gordon

Back in 1905, the Grand Trunk station agent lived in a house attached to the railway station at Brant Street and Plains Road. Gordon Blair's father was station agent at that time, so Gordon was born in that little house. When he was less than a year old, the station and dwelling were destroyed by fire. Young Gordon was carried to safety by Harry Copeland. The alarm was sounded, and Mr. Dunham had the horses attached to the fire engine even before the firemen arrived at the hall. By the time the firemen arrived, the station was almost completely consumed, so they devoted their efforts to saving nearby buildings owned by Mr. Renton, Mr. Fleetham and others. The loss was estimated at $1,500. Telegraphic instruments were installed in the tower, and a passenger car was placed on the property as a waiting room until the station could be replaced.

After this, the Blairs lived in the Hurd farmhouse on the corner of Brant and Birch Streets. When Gordon was growing up there, Brant Street was "an insignificant country road", and the population of the town was 1500.

As a young man, Gordon went on the road as a salesman for Maxwell Smith's Niagara brand chemicals. It was not an easy job, for during the Depression, farmers did not have the

Gordon Blair, (center) 1960. John Lockhart, Mayor.

Nelson Township Council, 1957. Warren McNiven, Wesel Gaul, Eric Gudgeon, Deputy Reeve, Lorne Lainge, Lou Dawson, John McCormack. Seated — Wm. Sims, clerk; Harold Atkins, reeve.

money to buy the things they needed. Gordon later referred to those years as "times of less hurry, with time to savour the pleasures of life."

In 1938, Gordon Blair was elected to town council, and in 1940 he became mayor of Burlington. The Depression was over, and the town's development was just beginning. The town had hundreds of acres of land taken over through tax sales, and lots sold for $50 on the condition that a house worth not less than $3,500 be built within the first year.

The town's development needed both direction and planning, so in 1959, with 20 years of experience behind him, Gordon Blair was chosen as the first director of business development. He was responsible for the first industrial park to be developed in Burlington. He was also a school board trustee, and chairman of the recreation commission, and of the public utility commission. Over the years, he held a number of posts with the Industrial Developers Association of Ontario, and chaired a committee on ethics and professionalism of the American Industrial Developers Council. He was also a co-founder of Burlington's first district hockey and softball leagues. He retired from his position with the city in 1975.

GUDGEON, Eric

One of the most crucial periods in Burlington's history was that of amalgamation when, in January of 1958, the new town of Burlington was formed from Nelson Township, Burlington, and the Aldershot area of East Flamborough. As a member of Nelson Township council, Eric Gudgeon had served on three committees — public works, finance and planning. This experience was invaluable when he worked on the committee that restructured the administration of the enlarged town. This included the consolidation of the fire and police departments, the boards of education, and water and hydro services.

Eric played a significant part in the field of education at this time. As chairman of the Joint Committee of Public School and High School Consultative Committees for Halton County, he directed the lengthy process of collecting and reporting

Rev. Thomas Webster Pickett & Mrs. Pickett, Keitha Pickett Henry & George S. Henry, Premier of Ontario, 1930-34, on the occasion of the Pickett's diamond wedding anniversary in 1933.

—*Courtesy Laura Dixon*

Victory Bond Parade on Brant St. with an unexploded V 1 Bomb, around 1945.

—*Courtesy Frank Armstrong*

Monument to those who served in the two World Wars.   —*Courtesy George Hawley*

data to the Ministry of Education and the Halton County Council. This resulted in the formation of the Halton Board of Education in January, 1969. Eric also served on the board which planned and executed the building of Nelson High School. As deputy reeve of Nelson Township, he was able to arrange for the issue of debentures to cover the township's share of the capital cost of the new school.

When Burlington residents began to press for the building of a local hospital, Eric Gudgeon was chosen as chairman of a committee to assess the situation and make recommendations. As a charter member of the Burlington-Nelson Hospital Association, he wrote the operating bylaws, and, with four others, signed the request for incorporation. In 1992, he was the only surviving signatory.

He was also chairman of the fund-raising committee which provided the basic financing for the original hospital. This was the first large fund-raising campaign ever held in Burlington and it was executed without help from professional fund-raisers. It exceeded its objective of $750,000! When the hospital was completed, Eric served in volunteer positions as chairman of the human relations committee, as an active member of both the finance and executive committees, and as a member of the Board of Governors.

For many years, he has supported the cause of local history in the community. He has served as president of the Burlington Historical Society. When the Joseph Brant Museum Board was formed, he became a member, and he is now a member of the new Burlington Museums Board. While wearing his historical preservation "hat", Erie took an active part in preserving both the Van Norman Homestead and the Ireland House which was purchased by the City of Burlington and is now a museum.

Eric Gudgeon has been active outside of Burlington, as well. He has served as both treasurer and chairman on the Board of Directors of the Chemical Institute of Canada. It is a tribute to his commitment and integrity that he was the first lay person to be appointed to the Royal College of Dental Surgeons of Ontario.

Ellis Hughes Cleaver, E. Hughes Cleaver, Jr.
Ivan Cleaver, around 1917.

—Courtesy Ivan Cleave

Dr. Norman Mitchell, naval doctor in Egypt. —Courtesy Ruth Mitchell Borthwick

PROFESSIONS

The pioneers who settled first in Nelson Township had no legal or medical services. There were only a few doctors, and no hospitals at all. Yet by the end of the 19th century, a Board of Health was set up in Nelson Township to supervise contagious diseases and control sanitary conditions. When smallpox came to the village in 1901, any citizen who wished could be vaccinated for 25 cents. The village paid the fee for those who could not afford it. When Mr. Pettigrew became ill with smallpox while visiting in the village, he was cared for at public expense in a tent set up in a field belonging to Wood Freeman. The total cost of this care was $295.70, including $20 to Mr. Freeman for the use of his field. Although the entire province suffered from the smallpox epidemic, Burlington had few cases, and no fatalities, a fact which is a tribute to the health services of the time.

In the early days, lawyers were also few and far between. Joseph Brant's grandson, Simcoe Kerr, practised law in Wellington Square before his death in 1875. At the time, he was the only lawyer in town, and for many years there were only two. After the Second World War, there were five lawyers in Burlington. By 1960, there were 11. In the mid 1970s, the Burlington Law Association and the Halton Law Association were formed. By 1990, the city had 85 lawyers, eight of them women.

DINGLE, Lloyd

For many years, R.W. Dingle (known to his friends as Dick) operated a butcher shop on the east side of Brant Street. His son Russell became a well-known doctor in town, while his other son, Lloyd, for many years practised law in Burlington.

Lloyd Dingle was born in 1899 and grew up in the village. He attended Osgoode Hall, and was called to the bar in 1923. Two years later, he became a King's Counsel. For many years, he and Hughes Cleaver were the only lawyers in town. There was naturally a good deal of rivalry between the two firms, probably heightened by the fact that Cleaver was a Liberal, while Dingle supported the Conservatives.

CLEAVER, Hughes

The busiest people always seem to get the most done. That certainly was true of Ellis Hughes Cleaver, called Hughes to differentiate from his father of the same name. Hughes Cleaver was a Burlington-born lawyer who became reeve of the town in 1918-19, and mayor in 1920.

He was involved in many ventures during his lifetime, many of them associated with his clients. One of these was the Bluebird bus line which ran from Hamilton to Toronto. The building that housed this business is still standing on John Street near Caroline. The main floor was used for servicing the buses, and the second floor housed a plant producing electrical fuses. The Bluebird line failed, in the end, because the Redbird bus line ran the same route and the competition was just too great.

Hughes Cleaver was an animal lover, and at another time, he had a fox farm on Caroline Street. Also, he became involved in a cure-all remedy called "radium water" which seemed promising until one user died and a police investigation followed.

Although Ross Hart laid out the Roseland area in 1922, it was Hughes Cleaver who actually developed Roseland Park, Roseland Court, Roseland Heights, and Shore Acres Heights surveys. The tree-lined streets of this area are due to Cleaver's policy of planting a Schwedler maple on each lot.

Roseland's name goes back more than a century and a half to the days when the Rev. and Mrs. Thomas Greene owned a large tract of land on Lakeshore Road just east of the Guelph Line. The property, called Highview, was famous for its beautiful display of roses, carefully tended by Mrs. Greene.

In 1929, Hughes Cleaver became associated with a company called English Inns Ltd. This organization planned to build four pseudo-thatched country inns — The Red Dragon in Grimsby (now Knudstrupp's Stained Glass studio), The Black Horse in Niagara Falls, The Pig and Whistle in Burlington, and a fourth which never materialized in Oakville. The Pig and Whistle was Cleaver's "baby". The Inn opened in the summer of 1930, with plans for operation each year from May to September. The place was beautiful, with a courtyard of matching cottages at the back. On opening day, two pipers marched in front of the Inn, and there was roast suckling pig on the dining room menu.

Unfortunately, the stock market crash and ensuing depression hit Cleaver hard. The Inn had to close at the end of its first season, and was put on the market for $30,000. Good ideas die hard, though, and the Inn was revived, becoming a popular place to dine or stay during the 1940s. The original cabins have been replaced by motel units, and the business still continues to-day. Through all its changes, it has retained its original name. It is interesting to note that the Grimsby inn building still has its courtyard of cottages at the rear.

During the crash of 1929, Hughes Cleaver lost all his money, and was heavily in debt. He fell into temptation, borrowing from clients without their permission. Consequently, he was disbarred by the Law Society. This was a case of history repeating itself, for Hughes' father, Ellis H. Cleaver, K.C., had a similar experience in pre-World War I days, although there is no record of him being disbarred. When Hughes could no longer practise, his father carried on the firm, working into his eighties.

In 1935, Hughes Cleaver decided to try a new career. He sought the federal Liberal party's nomination for the riding of Halton. At the nomination meeting, he made an impassioned speech, saying that since his disbarment, he had no other way of making a living. There were 15 candidates on the first ballot. On the third and final ballot, Hughes Cleaver won with 164 votes over Ed Harrop of Milton who had 129 and William Featherstone of Bronte who had 32. Hughes Cleaver was not only chosen as Liberal candidate, but also was elected, and served the community well from 1935 to 1953.

In spite of his financial difficulties, Hughes Cleaver never declared bankruptcy, and paid back all of the money he owed. In 1952, he was reinstated by the Law Society. It is said that in return for this, he promised not to run in the 1953 federal election.

During this period in his life, he returned to land development, laying out the subdivisions of Roseland Heights (the Bridgman farm), Longacres (the Long farm), and Highview. At his own expense, he had a tree planted on the front lawn of each home. He and his brother, Ivan, also went into real estate, building and selling affordable housing in Oakville. Ivan turned to the insurance business, insuring the homes they were selling.

FREEMAN, Dr. Claude

The village of Freeman, located at Brant Street and Plains Road, was named for the pioneer family who settled at this intersection early in the 19th century. Joshua Freeman's 400 acre farm was on the northwest corner of Brant Street and York Road (now Plains Road) on the site now occupied by Holland Motors. Later, Joshua's two sons farmed on both sides of the intersection, thus giving the thriving community its name. Freeman had its own post office, and the Freeman postmark continued to be used on mail until the 1960s.

In 1904, a member of this family, Dr. Claude Freeman, was appointed medical superintendent of Hamilton City Hospital. In her book, *The Hamilton General Hospital School of Nursing*, author Marjorie Freeman Campbell who was herself a member of this family, told the story of his brief tenure.

The year and a half that Dr. Freeman spent in his post was filled with turmoil. The lady superintendent of nurses, Carrie Bowman, resigned during this time due to the accusations of a former orderly who sent letters to the newspaper charging that under Miss Bowman's supervision, patients and staff were served with poor meals, and patients received inadequate care. The board of governors, which was also attacked in the letters, replied publicly, as did tradespeople who testified that they provided only the best quality supplies to the hospital. In the ensuing investigation, it was discovered "that milk, lemonade and ice for the wards were kept in bathrooms and bath tubs where utensils for typhoid cases were washed and stored." Nurses were accused of being "vain and frivolous, too fond of lovemaking."

Miss Bowman's successor was Isabella Grantham, a very qualified graduate of the Brooklyn Hospital. However, she apparently found that many of the former orderly's charges were true, for after only five months of dissension, she resigned.

Finally, Dr. Freeman could stand it no more. He handed his resignation to the board of governors, commenting that one of the problems was too frequent inspection visits to the hospital by the house committee. He suggested that one visit a week was enough, and that the committee should be accompanied by the medical superintendent. Although the board disagreed with Dr. Freeman's suggestions, they asked him to reconsider his resignation. He refused, saying, "I am tired of the whole business."

There was some compensation, however. Dr. Freeman married Florence Mortson, valedictorian of the hospital's graduating class of 1905. They moved to California to continue their medical careers.

MITCHELL, Dr. N.H.

In the 1920s, when Burlington was still a small town, a young doctor named Norman Hendrie Mitchell decided to set up his first practice here. Born in 1896 in Hamilton, he was the youngest of six children of Scottish parents who placed a high value on education. During the First World War, his medical training at the University of Toronto was interrupted by service with the Naval Medical Corps in the Mediterranean. After the war, he completed his medical studies, then took post-graduate training in Scotland.

Dr. Mitchell early on established his office and his home over LePatourel's drugstore on the east side of Brant Street.

Earlier, this had been the site of Burlington's first telephone exchange. Having no nurse or receptionist, Dr. Mitchell had his phone calls answered in the drugstore below. Even more remarkable is the fact that he never sent a bill to any patient. Patients paid what they could afford, although sometimes part of the payment was returned if the doctor thought it was too much! Some patients paid in kind, particularly at harvest time when many baskets of local produce found their way into the doctor's home. One patient, a professional artist, paid with one of his outstanding seascapes.

As a bachelor, Dr. Mitchell enjoyed breakfast at Paul Pendakias's restaurant around the corner on Water Street. Before going to his office, he would stop by the pop cooler in LePatourel's to discuss the stock pages of the newspaper with his friend, Elgin Harris.

One former patient said, "Dr. Mitchell was a psychiatrist without training, as well as a father to all." Patients invariably held him in high esteem. When Dr. Mitchell was terminally ill, Mrs. Victor Vallance of Lakehurst Villa bought him an air conditioner so that he could be more comfortable in the heat. After his death in 1969, she dedicated a room in the Joseph Brant Memorial Hospital to his memory. He did not die a wealthy man, in the usual sense of the word, but he was rich in the respect and affection of all who knew him.

GOODBRAND, Dr. J.S.

Dr. J.S. Goodbrand came to Burlington in 1938 to set up his practice. He was looking for a home that could also accommodate an office, and he soon believed that he had found it. The former Presbyterian manse on the northeast corner of Ontario and Hurd Streets was for sale for $2,800.

When Dr. Goodbrand went to see Ted Lucas, manager at the Royal Bank, he was refused a loan on the grounds that he had no credit rating. So the doctor drove to Flamborough Centre to see his friend, John Drummond, who lived on Pig Lane (now known more picturesquely as Garden Lane). After Dr. Goodbrand had explained his problem, Mr. Drummond said, "Just a minute," and disappeared upstairs. There was a good deal of thumping from the attic, and after a few minutes, Mr. Drummond appeared with the required cash. It had been hidden under the floor boards upstairs.

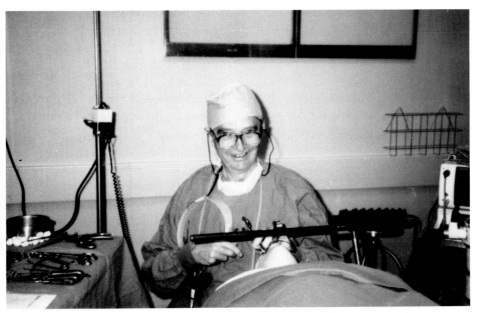

Dr. William Love

—Courtesy Dr. W. Love

Dr. Norman Mitchell during W.W. 1
—Courtesy Ruth Mitchell Borthwick

When Dr. Goodbrand began his practice, there was no hospital in Burlington, so he spent a great deal of the time driving to visit his patients in Hamilton hospitals. Many babies were still delivered at home.

Office hours were 2 to 4 p.m. and 7 to 8.30 p.m. from Monday to Saturday, and on Sundays from 1 to 2 p.m. There were few days off. Fees were $2 for an office call, and $4 for a house call. Many patients had no medical insurance, so that bills often went unpaid.

LOVE, Dr. William

For 40 years, one of the best-known names in medical circles in the area has been Love — an appropriate name for a family that has produced three outstanding doctors. Founder of this medical chronicle is Dr. William Love. A native of Hamilton, he admired his family doctor when he was a child, and resolved to follow in his footsteps.

After graduating from Delta Collegiate Institute, he attended medical school at Queen's University. His medical training was interrupted by a two year stint in the army's medical corps, at the request of the government of Canada, but he finally graduated as a doctor. Before returning to Hamilton to set up practice, young Dr. Love studied at the University of Iowa to become an ear, nose and throat specialist. His name became a household word as he removed tonsils, drained ears and performed many other important healings for local families. Colleagues referred to him as a masterful surgeon. Dr. Love admitted that he never used power tools in his home, as even a small injury could result in cancelling surgery for several weeks.

When Joseph Brant Memorial Hospital was built, Dr. Love became a supporter of the new institution, and was proud to be involved in its establishment. He moved his practice and his home to Burlington, retiring in 1990 after 40 years' service to the community.

The name Love will continue in Burlington's medical annals, however. Dr. Love's eldest son, William Jr., is chief of surgery at Joseph Brant Memorial Hospital. His son Robert is a surgeon in Kentucky. Two daughters live in Burlington.

Joseph Brant Memorial Hospital 1966. Joseph Brant Museum at left.
—*Courtesy Joseph Brant Museum.*

EPILOGUE

If the very earliest settlers — Joseph Brant, William Bates, Asahel Davis, David Fonger — could have become time travellers, they would have been astonished by turn-of-the-century Burlington. It would have seemed amazing to them to walk along Brant Street and see the many shops and businesses that were thriving there. The railways, the telephones, the automobiles that were just beginning to appear on the streets would have seemed incredible. Yet they would have recognized the lush fruit farms which gave the town its rural atmosphere, extending down Brant Street to within two blocks of the lake.

Even in the 1950s, our time travellers would have known that this growing Burlington was the same small town they had viewed in 1900. Although by then the community had begun to expand, with new industries appearing and farmland beginning to shrink, it was still essentially a "small town."

But if we bring those early settlers into the 1990s, they would be totally unable to relate this modern city with its malls, hotels and business complexes to the quiet, isolated community they knew.

The people in this book, and even those who came before them, all had roles to play in developing this city. Whether farmer, businessman, professional person, developer or ordinary working person, they all had dreams which bore fruit in one way or another. Few could have had any idea of the sort of community they were building. Each did the best he could to make the village, the town or the city into a place to be proud of.

This book is a tribute to all who have contributed in the past to making Burlington what it is to-day.

BIBLIOGRAPHY

Appleton, Gladys. *In Retrospect.*

Bailey, Thomas Melville, editor-in-chief. *Dictionary of Hamilton Biography.* Vol. 1, Hamilton, 1981.

Bridgman, Mrs. Clarence. *A History of Zimmerman and District, Ontario,* compiled in Centennial Year, 1967.

Clarke, Gwen. *Halton's Pages of the Past.* Dills Printing and Publishing Co., Acton, Ontario. 1955.

Campbell, Marjorie Freeman. *The Hamilton General Hospital School of Nursing,* The Ryerson Press, Toronto. 1956.

Campbell, Marjorie Freeman. *A Mountain and A City - The Story of Hamilton.* McLelland and Stewart, Toronto. 1966.

Coulter, Eleanor B. *This Old House - Fifty Years Ago. Memories of a Home.*

Emery, Claire; Ford, Barbara. *From Pathway To Skyway - A History of Burlington.* Confederation Centennial Committee of Burlington, 1967.

Fisher, Murray W. *Fisher Memories.* 1977.

Flatt, W.D. *Lakeshore Surveys.* 1912.

Flatt, W.D. *The Trail of Love.* William Briggs, Toronto. 1916.

Kelly, Percy A. M.B.E. *St. Luke's Church, Burlington, Ontario, 1834 - 1967.* 1973.

Langford, Helen. *Lindley Family History,* 1980.

McWilliams, Peter K. Q.C. *Rambling Tales of a Country Lawyer,* Milton, 1990.

Middleton, J.E.; Landon, Fred. *The Province of Ontario - A History.* 4 Vols. Dominion Publishing Co. Ltd. Toronto. 1927.

Morton, Jean. *A Historical Memorandum of A.S. Nicholson and Sons Ltd.* 1979.

Quigley, Michael. *On The Market.* 1987.

— *A History of the Church of St. Matthew-on-the-Plains - A Hundred Years, 1861 - 1961.*

Brass Tacks. Burlington Central High School. Vol. 1, No. 1, 1978 to Vol. 4, No. 2, 1982.

— *Sesquicentennial of The Parish Church of St. Luke - Wellington Square - Canada West, 1834.* Burlington, Ontario. 1984.

Scrapbooks prepared by Ariel Summers Kemp.

INDEX